That's life!

Alan Duff

Cambridge University Press

Cambridge
London New York New Rochelle
Melbourne Sydney

To Patrick Early

Published by the Press Syndicate of the University of Cambridge
The Pitt Building, Trumpington Street, Cambridge CB2 1RP
32 East 57th Street, New York, NY 10022, USA
296 Beaconsfield Parade, Middle Park, Melbourne 3206, Australia

First published 1979
Reprinted 1982

Designed by Peter Ducker

Printed in Great Britain by
Hazell Watson & Viney Ltd, Aylesbury, Bucks

ISBN 0 521 21916 7

Contents

Acknowledgements

The editor and publishers are grateful to the authors, publishers and others who have given permission for the use of copyright material identified in the text. It has not been possible to identify the sources of all the material used and in such cases the publishers would welcome information from copyright owners.
The cover cartoons from *This Pestered Isle* and the personal ads cartoon from the New Penguin *Calman* are used by kind permission of Mel Calman.
The Carl Sandburg extract from *The People, Yes*, copyright © 1936 by Harcourt Brace Jovanovich, Inc, copyright © 1964 by Carl Sandburg is reprinted by permission of the publishers; the article by Maeve Binchy is by permission of the author; all extracts from *The Observer* are by permission; Are You Good at Judging People is by permission of the *Evening Standard*; the extract from *The Politics of the Family* by R. D. Laing is by permission of Methuen & Co. Ltd; the extract from *Psychoanalysis and Religion* by Eric Fromm is by permission of Yale University Press; the puzzle is by permission of the *Daily Telegraph*; the extract from *Let My People Go* by Albert Luthuli is by permission of Collins Publishers; the extracts from *Sunset in Biafra* by E. Amadi and from *Fragments* by A. K. Armah are by permission of Heinemann Educational Books Ltd; the extract from *Bandiet*, published by Penguin, by Hugh Lewin, is by permission of Barrie and Jenkins; the extracts from *Serjeant Musgrave's Dance* by John Arden and *The House at Pooh Corner* by A. A. Milne and Upon My Word by Frank Muir and Dennis Norden (who wrote this story) are by permission of Eyre Methuen Ltd and Methuen Children's Books Ltd; the extracts from *The Concise Oxford Dictionary* and from *The Problems of Philosophy* by Bertrand Russell are by permission of Oxford University Press; the extract and cartoon from the *Book of Bores* are by permission of Private Eye; all articles from *The Times* and *Sunday Times* are by permission; all

articles from *The Guardian* are by permission; articles from the *Holburn and Ainsbury Guardian* are by permission of Fleet Street News Agency Ltd; the extracts from *Medical Terminology in Hospital Practice* by P. Davies, and *Medical Terms, their Origin and Construction* by F. Roberts are by permission of William Heinemann Medical Books Ltd; the extract from *Briefing for a Descent into Hell* by Doris Lessing is reprinted by permission of the author and Jonathan Cape Ltd; the extracts from *Fun-tastic* by Dennis Parsons are by permission of Pan Books; the extract on TM is by permission of Dell Publishing Co. Inc; the extract from *The Age of Enlightenment* is by permission of the Maharashi International College; the extract from The *Horizon Book of Lost Worlds* by Leonard Cottrell is reprinted by permission © 1962 American Heritage Publishing Company Inc; the extracts from *Civilisation* by Kenneth Clark, *Heat and Dust* by Ruth Prawer Jhabvala, and *Parkinson's Law* by C. Northcote Parkinson are by permission of John Murray (Publishers) Ltd; the extracts from *The Green Years* by Peter Abrahams are by permission of John Farquharson Ltd; the piece by Fred Hoyle from *The Nature of the Universe* is by permission of Curtis Brown; the extracts from *Zen and the Art of Motorcycle Maintenance* by Robert Pirsig published by The Bodley Head are by permission of Laurence Pollinger Ltd; *It* is by permission of Souvenir Press Ltd; The Chair and The Ceiling from *The Collected Poems of Theodore Roethke* are by permission of Faber and Faber Ltd; the piece about the Reith Lectures by Ian McEwan, and about The Blues, by Stanley Reynolds, are by permission of Radio Times; the extracts from *Straight and Crooked Thinking* by Robert Thouless are by permission of Hodder and Stoughton Educational; the piece from *Witcracks* is by permission of A. Schwartz and Pan Books; the extract from *The Unconscious Mind* by Kenneth Walker is by permission of Hutchinson Publishing Group Ltd; Bishop Raps Sexy Ads is by permission of Syndication International Ltd; articles from the *South Kensington and Chelsea News* are by permission of London Newspaper Group; all articles from the *Daily Telegraph* are by permission; The Bee by Peter Kelso is from *Once Around the Sun* published by OUP Australia; the extract from *History of England* by E. L. Woodward is by permission of

Methuen & Co. Ltd; the Giles cartoon is by permission of *The Sunday Express*; the articles from the *Hampstead and Highgate Express* are by permission; the article from *Which?* is used by permission of the publishers, Consumers' Association; the extract from *The Status Seekers* by Vance Packard is reprinted by permission of the David Mackay Company Inc copyright © 1959 by Vance Packard; the extract from *The Political Education of Clarissa Forbes* by Shiva Naipaul is by permission of Curtis Brown; the piece from *The City Machine* is © 1972 by Louis Trimble by permission of Daw Books Inc; I Wonder who's Kissing her now? © 1909 is reproduced by permission of Francis Day and Hunter Ltd; the piece from *Sweet Dreams* by Michael Frayn is by permission of Collins Publishers; the piece on Southern Comfort and the blues from an advertisement in *The Sunday Times Magazine* is by permission of Clode Baker & Wyld Ltd; the extract from *Beneath the Underdog* by Charles Mingus is by permission of Weidenfeld & Nicolson; articles from the *Daily Mail* are by permission; the advertisement from Smirnoff Vodka is by permission of International Distillers and Vintners; the application for a driving licence is Crown copyright, reproduced by permission of the Controller of Her Majesty's Stationery Office; the extract from *Under the Volcano* by Malcolm Lowry is by permission of the executors of the Malcolm Lowry Estate and Johnathan Cape Ltd; the piece by James Stern originally published in *Encounter* is copyright © 1967 by James Stern; the piece from *Understanding Children Writing* is copyright © Carol Burgess and co-authors 1973, by permission of Penguin Books Ltd; the extract from *To Sir, With Love*, by E. R. Braithwaite is by permission of The Bodley Head; the illustrations from *The House at Pooh Corner* are by permission of Curtis Brown on behalf of the estate of E. H. Shephard; the extract from *For Whom the Bell Tolls* by E. Hemingway is by permission of Jonathan Cape on behalf of the executors of the Ernest Hemingway estate; the articles from the *Sun* are by permission of London Express News and Feature Services.

Introduction

That's life! is a book for private reading and enjoyment. And private reading does not necessarily mean sitting down at a desk with a dictionary in one hand and a notebook at the other!

One of the best ways to enjoy a book like this is to look through it, reading what you *feel* like reading at that particular moment. There is no need at all to begin at page 1 – begin where you like, read what you like and go at your own speed.

What is in the book

The book is made up of short passages drawn from many different sources – newspapers, notice boards, reports, brochures, advertisements, magazines, novels, posters, letters, etc. Each passage is separate and can be read on its own. All the same, there is a link – often a strong one – between texts. The headings to each section suggest what the passages may have in common (for example, *Cashing in* contains many texts on moneymaking, *The green years* deals with children, particularly at the age when they begin to go to school). Often, this link is not between two passages but several, for instance in the section *Short tales and tall stories*, a passage from 'Winnie the Pooh' is followed by a passage from Hemingway, which in turn is followed by a satirical piece called 'The Pooh Also Rises'.

The internal arrangement of the book, however, is one of convenience. The passages had to occur in some order, and this is the order they were given. The context in which they originally appeared may well have been very different. This is why you should feel free to use the book as you like.

Each passage in this book has a style of its own, a character of its own. And each is authentic, in that it was written to be understood by English-speakers. Very few changes have been made to the character of the original. Some passages have been shortened, but wherever possible the style and wording of the original has been kept.

Strange words

When reading, remember that *meaning* is not carried by words alone. It is often possible to understand part of a passage without being able to 'explain' the words. This is not as strange as it may sound. Consider, for instance, the remarkable passage by Malcolm Lowry in the section *One for the road*, made up almost entirely of 'foreign' words. From the opening sentences we know that the author is thinking back (without regret!) over a long life of drinking, and that he imagines the empty bottles as a tower of glass about to fall on him: 'aguardiente, anís, jerez, Highland Queen, Pernod, absinthe, Dubonnet . . .' The effect is made. The fact that you may not know what aguardiente *means* or *is*, does not seriously harm your understanding of the passage.

Similarly, you may not need to know more than the text tells you. The word *budgerigar* is one you may never have met. Yet, in the following sentence from the regulations for entry into Great Britain, you are told enough to be able to read on without difficulty: 'Birds of the parrot family (for example, budgerigars) may be freely imported into Great Britain.' Only the reader who actually intends to import 'birds of the parrot family' into Great Britain need know more.

Explanations

Wherever difficult words or special references occur, these are glossed, that is, marked with a sign (°) and explained at the end of the passage. Try first to read without using the glosses at all. If you notice that a word is marked, try to find your own meaning for it. Then check with the gloss when you have *finished* the passage. You will often find that the context has helped you to understand the word. With some words and phrases, of course, this is not possible. Technical words and specialized expressions, eg *breathalyse*, *girder*, *transcendental meditation*, may be difficult to work out from the context.

Likewise, familiar words used in an unusual sense may give difficulty, e.g. *bread*, meaning money; *well-heeled*, meaning rich. These, however, are usually glossed and explanations of the particular usage (legal, botanical, slang, idiomatic, etc.) are given in brackets. Where necessary, an editorial note has been added, marked with an asterisk (*).

Thanks

I should like to thank the embassies of Australia, Canada and Great Britain in Belgrade, and Chris Harrison of the British Council for help in providing me with much useful material.

Paris, October 1977 A.D.

1 Men and masks

A man is not just himself. He is a combination of everyone he has met.

(A. S. Neill)

*

What Paul says about Peter tells us more about Paul than about Peter.

(Spinoza)

*

There is a continuous cold war between me and my clothes.

(Malcolm Lowry)

*

Show me a man's friends and I'll tell you who he is.

(Dr Johnson?)

What kind of a liar are you?

What kind of a liar are you?
People lie because they don't remember clear* what they saw.
People lie because they can't help making a story better than it was the way it happened.
People tell 'white lies'° so as to be decent to others.
People lie in a pinch°, hating to do it, but lying on because it might be worse.
And people lie just to be liars for a crooked° personal gain.
What sort of a liar are you?
Which of these liars are you?

(Carl Sandburg)

white lies: harmless lies
in a pinch: when hard pressed, in difficulties
crooked: dishonest

**Editorial note:* should be adverb 'clearly'.

PERSONAL COLUMN

●**6ft 2in,** happy male, 30, toe-tickler°, seeks SIMILAR FEMALE with pretty feet, to tickle away the cold winter evenings.
●**SINGLE** guy, own home, sports car. Wishes to meet natural-looking female, jeans-clad°. Interests: old films, music.
●**ENGLISHMAN** (30), quiet, attractive, tired of denim-clad°, combat-jacketed° girls, seeks more femininely attired° woman.
●**SERBO-CROAT AND JAPANESE**-speaking girls sought° by English graduate, 29, for friendship and help with languages.

(*Time Out*)

JOAN forgive us. Please contact us. Anita, Billy and Barry.
BYNOE, Walter Sinclair, father of Marion Gordon, or anyone knowing his whereabouts°, please contact Vic Brazeau 221–1161

(*Toronto Globe & Mail*)

MALE, young 42, entertainment club director, luxury Tudor-style Surrey residence°, wishes to contact attractive lady 20–35, pen friend to commence°, later possibly to run and reside in his residence. Sincere, genuine replies only. Lovely home to right person. Photo please to Box 38387.

(*Hampstead & Highgate Express and News*)

tickler/tickle: touch skin lightly to make someone laugh
jeans-clad/denim-clad: wearing jeans
combat-jacketed: wearing old army jackets
femininely attired: dressed like a woman
sought: wanted
whereabouts: where he is living or working
residence: large house
commence: begin

Gentleman with artistic tastes
and cold feet
wishes to meet lady with
property in Bermuda . . .

(Calman)

Nobody's watching me

I am a foot taller than Napoleon and twice the weight of Twiggy°; on my only visit to a beautician, the woman said she found my face a challenge°. Yet despite these social disadvantages I feel cheerful, happy, confident and secure.

I work for a daily newspaper and so get to a lot of places I would otherwise never see. This year I went to Ascot° to write about the people there. I saw something there that made me realise the stupidity of trying to conform° – of trying to be better than anyone else. There was a small, plump° woman, all dressed up – huge hat, dress with pink butterflies, long white gloves. She also had a shooting-stick°. But because she was so plump, when she sat on the stick it went deep into the ground and she couldn't pull it out. She tugged° and tugged, tears of rage in her eyes. When the final tug brought it out, she crashed with it to the ground.

I saw her walk away. Her day had been ruined. She had made a fool of herself in public – she had impressed nobody. In her own sad, red eyes she was a failure.

I remember well when I was like that, in the days before I learned that nobody really cares what you do. There were years of trying to be like other people, of useless worrying about what people were thinking about me. Now I know they weren't thinking about me at all.

I remember the pain of my first dance, something that is always meant to be a wonderful starry occasion for a girl, or so the rubbishy° magazines which we read told us. There was a fashion then for diamanté° ear-rings, and I wore them so often practising for the big night that I got two great sores on my ears and had to put sticking-plaster on them. Perhaps it was this that made nobody want to dance with me. Whatever it was, there I sat for four hours and 43 minutes. When I came home, I told my parents that I had a marvellous time and that my feet were sore from dancing. They were pleased at my success and they went to bed happy, and I went to my room and tore the bits of sticking-plaster off my ears and cried all night because I thought that, in 100 homes, people were telling their parents that nobody had danced with me.

One day, I was sitting in a park, worrying as usual whether I would look foolish sitting there by myself if any of my friends passed by, when I began reading a passage from a French essay. There was a line about a woman who was always wishing away° the present and dreaming of the future, just as I was always doing. Apparently, the woman spent most of her time trying to impress people, and very little actually living her life. At that moment, I realised that my whole 20 years had been spent running a useless race. It didn't matter what I did, because nobody was watching me.

I suddenly knew that the next time I went into a shop, and an assistant curled up her lip and said, 'In *your* size, Madam? Oh no, I don't think we would have anything like that,' it just meant that the shop was not properly stocked°. It was as if someone had lifted a great weight from my chest; I felt lighter and freer than I ever remembered having felt.

(Maeve Binchy, *The Listener*)

Twiggy: well-known model, famous for her thinness
challenge: difficult task
Ascot: large, fashionable horse-race track
conform: be like everyone else
plump: rather fat
shooting-stick: metal or wooden stick, sharply pointed at one end, with a small seat at the other
tugged: pulled hard
rubbishy: not worth reading
diamanté: imitation diamond
wishing away: not wanting
stocked: supplied

RELATIONSHIPS

to meet compatible° people
contact

Yvonne Allen and Associates
Human Relations Consultants
63–65 Crown St, East Sydney

(Advertisement)

compatible: people who one can get on with well, sympathetic, likeable

'I THOUGHT THEY WERE JOKING
when they asked me to take a computer° test to find my perfect partner . . .'

'That's just not on°,' I said, 'computers are okay for travel bookings, hotel reservations and that sort of thing . . . but really . . . when it comes to choosing personal relationships, I want something a little more warm-blooded than a box of printed circuits!°'

'Oh, come on, how on earth could you ever find that someone . . . that special someone out there who likes to do all the sort of things that you like to do, go to the sort of places you like to go, and a hundred other things besides.'

'Yes, well, you don't quite understand. You see, in a way, I'm a bit special, not being big-headed° or anything, but I am a bit particular in a way about people I meet and things I like . . .'

'So am I and so are thousands of others – just like you! You see, the computer is just a way to get you introduced. In fact Dateline have over 80,000 members right now – people of all ages, all kinds of jobs, all sorts of interests. So there's got to be someone you would really like . . . besides, computer introductions are more warm-blooded than you think. Some have led to spontaneous° affairs, some to pleasant relationships and others to firm, lasting friendships – even marriage! . . . Now, what are you waiting for? You've got nothing to lose. Meeting new people and making new friends is going to change your whole way of life. Why don't you send in for the free computer test today?'

'O.K. I'll give it a go°.'

(Advertisement for Dateline International, London)

computer: machine for solving complicated problems
not on: I can't accept it
circuits: wires, tubes, channels
big-headed: proud, self-important
spontaneous: natural
give it a go: (colloquial) try

Is your slip showing°?

What do you do when a really attractive person corners you with an interested stare?

You are on a bus, at the library, in a pub or walking on a crowded pavement and a pair of eyes seize you. I'll bet that every one of you who coolly acts as if you do not notice, kick yourself when you get home.

It's similar to posing for a photograph. Do you tighten up your face, hunch° your shoulders and grin and bear it? Or can you take a deep relaxing breath and look straight at the camera?

More often than not we are feeling quiet, perhaps a bit unsure of ourselves, and the glance of a perfect stranger will set us thinking, 'Oh, heavens, I *do* look terrible today!' or 'Why can't I be left alone with my thoughts!' So, what can you do when that tall handsome someone smashes you with a look?

Automatically, assume that he enjoys looking at you. Don't pretend that you have not seen, because whoever is admiring you will take that as a snub°, and might be brave enough to return it! At the same time, your response should be slow, warm and tactful, so as not to frighten the admirer. The hunter, after all, can be more skittish° than the prey°.

(*Single Scene*)

is your slip showing?: is your behaviour too obvious
hunch: pull in
snub: rejection
skittish: nervous, frightened
prey: animal hunted for food

The taxes of sin

No-one knows the woman I love.
The woman knows I love no-one.
I love no-one the woman knows.
The woman knows no-one I love.
No-one knows I love the woman.
I love the woman no-one knows.
No-one I love knows the woman.
The woman no-one knows I love.
(Alan Maley)

CAPRICORN (21 December–19 January)

(a) A very energetic time coming up when you could make some much-needed extra cash°. Don't worry if others won't accept your ideas. You know you're on a winner°.

(b) Plans for an exciting social event or outing are in the air which will give you something to look forward to and to plan.

(c) Expect to be in very big demand socially. Letters or phone calls suggesting that you embark° on a romantic relationship should be approached with caution – such a situation can lead to trouble from relatives who disapprove. All important decisions should be deferred°.

TAURUS (21 April–20 May)

(a) You may notice nice qualities in people you work with. And others become much more aware of you. Don't let this distract° you completely from work or business. Just enjoy your great popularity.

(b) You could get your own back° on someone who is trying to cause trouble between yourself and your romantic partner. Follow the advice of an older person.

(c) There are gains to be made in business and intimate situations but not before old differences of opinion have been settled. It seems that you will have to be more flexible° in your approach than you have been recently, but you have much to gain if you make a special effort now.

VIRGO (22 August–22 September)

(a) You may stumble on° a super idea. And this may make money for you. Your good business sense reaches a peak° after midday. Mix it with imagination and you can't go wrong.

(b) Some sort of conflict° is indicated in your social life which could cause trouble between yourself and a close friend. The initial 'C' has a special significance.

(c) You may have fears about close relatives. Avoid unnecessary worry. Fortunately, you may also find yourself leading an exciting social life. This is not typical of Virgo, but in the circumstances it is an opportunity not to be missed.

(*a*) *The Sun*, 2 November 1976
(*b*) *Camden & St Pancras Chronicle*, 5 November 1976
(*c*) *Prima*, November 1976

cash: money
on a winner: in a good position
embark: start
deferred: put off
distract: draw one's attention away
get your own back: (idiomatic) have your revenge
flexible: willing to change
stumble on: discover by chance
peak: high point
conflict: struggle

Miss World

After a promising start involving such cosmic° issues as race, politics and the United Nations, the Miss World competition is once again declining° to its usual boobs° and bottoms banality°.

The disqualification° of Miss Transkei before she had set foot on British soil (Transkei, pointed out the Mecca Organisation, is not internationally recognised) did not arouse much sympathy among the other contestants. One of them thought the Transkei was a boutique° in Chelsea.

The organisers at Mecca have not relaxed their hold on the girls, who are encouraged to talk only about make-up and how much they like London. An army of chaperones°, female, stands ready to protect the girls from trick questions like Do you think Mrs Thatcher could ever have become Miss World?

Everyone wants to meet Miss Australia, a favourite for the title – and, besides, her English is quite good. No one could do much with the breathtakingly exotic° Miss Turkey because no one, not even the interpreter, spoke Turkish. 'So what do you do in Turkey?' asked a middle-aged man, 'I admire the spirit of your young people,' she replied gravely°.

(*The Observer*)

cosmic: universal, of world importance
declining: sinking
boobs: (vulgar) breasts
banality: stupidity, emptiness
disqualification: non-acceptance
boutique: smart shop
chaperones: guardians
exotic: striking, unusual
gravely: seriously

Are you good at judging people?

A. Which of the following characteristics would you most readily connect with each face:

1. (*a*) rapture°
(*b*) anxiety°
(*c*) surprise

2. (*a*) resignation°
(*b*) submission°
(*c*) surprise

3. (*a*) disdain°
(*b*) anger
(*c*) joy

4. (*a*) grief°
(*b*) anger
(*c*) distaste

5. (*a*) irritation°
(*b*) anxiety
(*c*) mistrust

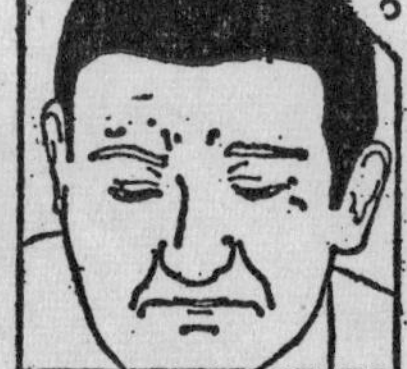

6. (*a*) fear
(*b*) sentimentality
(*c*) concentration

B. Which of the following qualities would you most readily connect with each of these three faces:

1–3. (*a*) matter-of-factness°
(*b*) sociability
(*c*) toughness

C. Which one of the writing samples most readily indicates that the writer is a good mixer? (top, middle, or bottom?)

summer
simmer
simmer

Answers: A. 1, *c*; 2, *b*; 3, *a*; 4, *b*; 5, *c*; 6, *b*.
B. 1, *c*; 2, *a*; 3, *b*.
C. top.

(Angus McGill, *Evening Standard*)

rapture: delight, great joy
anxiety: worry
resignation: accepting a situation because you cannot change it
submission: giving in to someone stronger
disdain: scorn, pride
grief: great unhappiness
irritation: annoyance, anger over small matters
matter-of-factness: directness, simplicity

```
amiwhoiam
   who
   who
   who
   who
   who
   who
   who
   who
   who
   who
amiwhoiam
```

```
WHOam         amWHO          WHOamamamamam
WHO am       am WHO          WHOamamamamam
WHO  am     am  WHO          WHO
WHO   am   am   WHO          WHO
WHO    am am    WHO          WHO
WHO      i      WHO          WHOami
WHO             WHO          WHO
WHO             WHO          WHO
WHO             WHO          WHO
WHO             WHO          WHOamamamamam
WHO             WHO          WHOamamamamam
```

```
are        are      AREYOU      you    you
 are      are      WHO  ARE     you    you
  are    are      YOU    YOU    you    you
   are  are       are    are    you    you
    areare        are    are    you    you
      WHO         are    are    you    you
      WHO         are    are    you    you
      WHO         are    are    you    you
      WHO         are    are    you    you
      WHO         YOU    YOU    ARE    WHO
      WHO          WHO  ARE      WHO  ARE
      WHO           AREYOU        YOUARE
```

WHOAMIAMIWHOIAMWHOIAM

YOUWHOAREWHO

WHOWHO

WHOYOUWHOAREYOUWHOAREWHOAREYOU

AMWHOIAMWHOIAMA

AWWHOAMWHOIAMWHO

IAMWHOIAMWHOIAMWHOIAMWHO

AMWHOIAMIAMWHOAMWHOIAM

AMIAMIAMWHOIAMWHOIAM

AMWHOIAMWHOIAMWHO

AMWHOIAM

I AM

I guess that by one year from birth the following distinctions, among others, have come to be made.

(1) *Inside and outside*
(2) *Pleasure and pain, pleasant–unpleasant*
(3) *Real and not-real*
(4) *Good and bad*
(5) *Me and not-me*
(6) *Here and there*
(7) *Then and now*

I slice° my experience into inside–outside: real–unreal: good and bad: me and not-me: here and there: now and then; I find it pleasant or painful.

One of our fundamental distinctions is inside and outside. It cannot be considered for long in isolation° from the other distinctions we make: this distinction (as all others) operates with other distinctions according to rules for their combination. The inside–outside distinction is applied to almost all facets° of experience.

Imagine the following actions:

(1) *swallow the saliva° in your mouth*;
(2) *take a glass of water: sip it and swallow it*;
(3) *spit in it, swallow spit and water*;
(4) *sip some water: spit it back, sip and swallow what you have spat back.*

You may be able to do all four, easily, but many people cannot, and are disgusted° especially at (3) and (4).

One is aware that there is a difference between saliva inside one's mouth, and that same saliva, one centimetre in space outside one's mouth.

We feel ourselves to be inside a bag of skin: what is outside this bag is not-us. Me – inside. Not-me – outside.

(R. Laing, *The politics of the family*)

slice: cut up
isolation: complete separation
facets: sides
saliva: liquid produced inside the mouth
disgusted: made to feel sick

In a recent survey two questions were asked of whites in the North and South of the United States: 1. Are all men created equal? 2. Are the Negroes equal to the Whites? Even in the South 61 per cent answered the first question in the affirmative° but only 4 per cent answered the second question in the affirmative. (For the North the figures were 79 per cent and 21 per cent, respectively)°. The person who assented° only to the first question undoubtedly remembered it as a thought learned in classes and retained it because it is still part of a generally recognized, respectable ideology°, but it has no relation to what the person really feels: it is, as it were, in his head, without any connection with his heart and hence° without any power to influence his action. A survey today in the United States would show almost complete unanimity° that democracy is the best form of government. But this does not prove that all those who expressed an opinion in favour of democracy would fight for it if it were threatened.

Any idea is strong only if it is grounded in a person's character structure.

(Erich Fromm, *Psychoanalysis and religion*)

answered in the affirmative . . .: said yes
respectively: each
assented: agreed
ideology: guiding belief
hence: so
unanimity: agreement

Change 'hate' to 'love'

If you like word puzzles try these new ones by Edward de Bono. What you have to do is to change one word into another, one letter at a time – but you must not change more than one letter at each stage. The new word formed at each stage must be a recognised English word in ordinary use. No proper nouns or foreign words, please.

Solution to last week's puzzle: change

MESS to TIDY (ten moves); change SICK to WELL (eight moves)

SICK	MESS
NICK°	MISS
NICE	MIST
MICE	FIST
MILE	FISH
MILL	WISH
SILL°	WISE
SELL	RISE
WELL	RIDE
	TIDE
	TIDY

This week's puzzle: change HATE to LOVE

(*The Sunday Telegraph Magazine*)

nick: make a small cut
sill: outside lower edge of a window

Which route to freedom?

The present situation, if I may put it in a parable°, seems to me something like this. My next-door neighbour and I may like each other or we may not. At all events°, we shall, if we are normal people, pay attention to the social conventions°. We shall mind our own business unless invited to do otherwise. We shall not interfere with each other's wife or children or property. We shall avoid abusive° language and greet each other when we meet.

But a day might come when this relationship breaks down. I might happen to glance across to his lands and see him savagely whipping° a member of his household or attacking a defenceless child with a lethal° weapon. I might learn that he has done his brother to death°.

I could shrug° and go my way. I could say, 'Well, after all, he's the head of the household, it's no business of mine. I don't want him interfering here, so I'd better keep myself to myself.' Or I suppose I could go round to the door and leave a little note suggesting that it might be wise if he were to make a few changes in his behaviour, and then leave him to think it all over.

But I doubt if I would be morally justified° in taking any further course except doing my utmost to prevent his doing any further damage. My aim would not be to kill or injure him. It would be to stop him.

(Albert Luthuli, '*Let my people go*')

parable: a story with a moral lesson
at all events: anyway, whatever happens
conventions: customs, rules
abusive: rude
whipping: beating
lethal: deadly
done . . . to death: killed
shrug: lift the shoulders to show indifference or doubt
justified: in the right

UNIVERSAL DECLARATION OF HUMAN RIGHTS

Article **1** All human beings are born free and equal in dignity° and rights. They are endowed with° reason and conscience° and should act towards one another in a spirit of brotherhood.
Article **2** Everyone is entitled to° all the rights and freedoms set forth in this Declaration, without distinction° of any kind, such as race, colour, sex, language, religion, political or other opinion, national or social origin, property, birth or other status.
Article **3** Everyone has the right to life, liberty and security of person.
Article **5** No one shall be subjected to torture° or to cruel, inhuman or degrading° punishment.
Article **6** Everyone has the right to recognition everywhere as a person before the law.
Article **13** Everyone has the right to freedom of movement and residence° within the borders of each state.

Everyone has the right to leave any country, including his own, and to return to his country.
Article **15** Everyone has the right to a nationality.
Article **17** Everyone has the right to own property alone as well as in association with others.
Article **18** Everyone has the right to freedom of thought, conscience and religion; this right includes freedom to change his religion or belief.
Article **19** Everyone has the right to freedom of opinion and expression.
Article **23** Everyone has the right to work, to free choice of employment, to just and favourable conditions of work, and to protection against unemployment. Everyone, without discrimination°, has the right to equal pay for equal work.

(UN, Office of Public Information, quoted in *Rights and wrongs*, ed. Christopher Hill)

dignity: personal worth
endowed with: given
conscience: (1) understanding of right and wrong, (2) belie
entitled to: allowed
distinction: difference
torture: cause severe physical or mental suffering
degrading: shameful
residence: living
discrimination: making unfair differences between men

from **Sunset in Biafra**

'Put down your bag,' he said. 'I want to search you.'

I obeyed. He rummaged° through my handbag.

'Strip!°'

'Surely you can search me without my stripping?'

'Strip!'

I removed my shirt.

'Off with your trousers!'

'What is all this?'

'Off with your trousers, I say!'

The detainees° looked at me sadly. There were three women among them. One of them had a child of about three with her. She sighed.

I removed my trousers.

'Now search me,' I said coldly.

'Off with your pants!'

I was surprised. I did not move. Anger began to well up° in me. I fought to control it.

'Do you suppose I can hide a gun inside my pants?'

'Off with your pants, I say!'

There was silence. My fellow detainees watched in frozen attention.

He cocked° his machine-gun and pointed it at my legs. The fellow might shoot to save his pride; not to kill, perhaps, but to injure. It had happened many times already.

'Now strip, I say.'

I stripped.

'Now have a good look,' I said. 'Does it compare with your father's.'

The detainees could not help giggling°. The guard could not reply.

(Elechi Amadi, *Sunset in Biafra*)

rummaged: hunted
strip: undress
detainees: prisoners
well up: rise
cocked: prepared (for shooting)
giggling: laughing

Solitary

Walking into prison is like walking into a butcher's fridge, empty. It is cold – no curtains, no carpets, no heaters, nothing decorative°, nothing unnecessary, just this long, dull corridor with heavy doors, impersonal – and all very solid. Essentials only. You are stripped° of everything inessential. You are stripped bare and given back only what they think is necessary. They strip you at the beginning and they go on stripping you, endlessly, to ensure that you have only what they think is necessary. You are stripped bare of everything that you can call your own, constantly stripped bare in an endless process of peeling° off your protective covering and leaving you naked. So that they can watch you. So that you, like the corridor, are without decoration, without covering, with nothing behind which to hide, with nothing they can't see into and watch.

'Strip,' said the man with three stripes on his arm°. He was alone in his office. He looked at me through half-closed eyes, and said, 'Strip'.

So I started to strip, article by article, thinking only of the pencil in my one sock and the ballpoint in the other. I could feel them pressing against my legs as I tried to steady my bag on the floor between my legs. He took my overcoat and began to go through the pockets. 'What's this?' – he held up the tiny set of cards I'd made from a toothpaste box.

'A pack of cards,' I said brightly.

'What for?'

'To play with,' I said. 'There's not much to do in a cell, you know.'

(Hugh Lewin, *Bandiet*)

decorative: bright, coloured
stripped: made to undress and give over everything you have on you
peeling: removing (like the skin of a fruit)
stripes . . .: sign of his rank in the police force

ADVERTISEMENT

1976

A year of double talk°

As the New Year approaches evidence has piled up that the world has been living on double standards and double talk in 1976.

Early in 1976, Leonard Garment, the chief US delegate to the United Nations, declared that the United Nations Commission on Human Rights had become a travesty°.

Torture° of prisoners

In August, the Secretary General of the International Committee of Jurists°, Mr Niall MacDermott, submitted° a document accusing eight countries of torturing political prisoners. This document was distributed to members during a meeting in Geneva of a United Nations committee drawing up a report on discrimination°.

When it was seen that the jurists' charges were supported by details of individual cases of torture, there was uproar°.

They were accused of being a CIA° organisation and Mr MacDermott of being a CIA agent.

Mr MacDermott replied that torture was a worldwide problem, and it must be made clear which countries practised it, otherwise a report would be useless.

Thousands in jails

How widespread is man's inhumanity° to man was shown towards the end of the year by the annual report of Amnesty International.

This accused more than 100 countries throughout the world of having imprisoned people for their beliefs, denied them fair trials and tortured or executed° them during 1975–76.

During this period, Amnesty International took up°

the cases of no fewer than 1,880 prisoners in 113 countries.

'More than 40 governments around the world have removed the individual's rights of expression and freedom, or, worse, have engaged in some hideous° form of torture of their citizens.'

(The Club of Ten, London)

double talk: saying one thing and doing another
travesty: ridiculous
torture: causing great physical suffering
Jurists: lawyers
submitted: gave in
discrimination: unfair treatment of a race or group of people
uproar: noisy protest
CIA: American secret intelligence service
inhumanity: cruelty
executed: put to death
took up: examined
hideous: frightful horrible

---

from **Serjeant Musgrave's dance**

(In a small country town in the North of England, the Mayor, the Priest (parson) and Serjeant Musgrave are trying to persuade the men to join the Army.)

PARSON: 'And Jesus said, I come not to bring peace but a sword.' I know very well that the times are difficult. As your minister of religion it is my business to be aware of these matters. But we must remember that this town is only one very small locality° in our great country.

BARGEE: Very true, very true.

(Two cheers off)

PARSON: And if our country is great, and I for one am sure that it *is* great, it is great because of the greatness of its responsibilities. They are world wide. They are noble. They are the responsibilities of a first-class power.

BARGEE: Keep 'em there°, Reverend! First-class for ever! Give a cheer, you boys!

(Three weak cheers)

And the crowd roars! Every hat in the air, you've struck 'em in the running nerve°, hooroar!

PARSON: Therefore, I say, therefore: when called to shoulder our country's burdens°, we should do it with a glancing° eye and a leaping heart, to draw the sword with gladness, thinking nothing of our petty° differences – but all united under one brave flag, going forth in Christian resolution, and showing a manly spirit! The Empire calls! Greatness is at hand! Serjeant Musgrave will take down the names of any men willing, if you'll file on the platform° in an orderly fashion, in the name of the Father, the Son, and mumble mumble mumble . . .°

MUSGRAVE: (his voice very taut and hard) The question remains as to the *use* of these weapons! (He pushes in his rifle-bolt.) You'll ask me: what's their purpose? Seeing° we've beat the Russians in the Crimea, there's no war with France (there *may* be, but there isn't yet), and Germany's our friend, who do we have to fight? *Well*, the Reverend answered that for you in his good short words. Me and my three lads° – we belong to a regiment that's a few thousand miles from here, in a little country without much importance, except from the point of view that there's a Union Jack° over it and the people of that country can write British Subject after their names. And that makes us proud!

ATTERCLIFFE: I tell you it makes us proud!

HURST: We live in tattered° tents in the rain, we eat rotten food, there's knives in the dark streets and blood on the floors of the hospitals, but we stand tall and proud: because of why we are there.

ATTERCLIFFE: Because we're there to serve our duty.

MUSGRAVE: A soldier's duty is a soldier's life.

(*A roll on the drum*)

A soldier's life is to lay it down, against the enemies of his Queen,

(*A roll on the drum*)

against the invaders of his home,

(*A roll on the drum*)

against slavery, cruelty, tyrants.

(*A roll on the drum*)

HURST: You put on the uniform and you give your life away, and who do you give it to?

ATTERCLIFFE: You give it to your duty.

MUSGRAVE: And you give it to your people, for peace and for honesty.

(John Arden, *Serjeant Musgrave's dance*)

locality: place
keep 'em there: go on
struck 'em . . .: you've touched their deepest feelings
burdens: responsibilities, tasks
glancing: bright
petty: little
file on the platform: come up (onto the wooden stage from which they are speaking)
mumble, mumble: the Parson is saying the words of the end of a prayer which he does not speak clearly
seeing: since
lads: his fellow-soldiers
Union Jack: the British flag
tattered: torn

He stood thoughtfully watching the rain driving across the plain below. It reminded him, every moment, more and more of England. After weeks of sun, of the long days of glittering° heat, the rain seemed almost unendurably° soft and friendly. And he knew as he watched it blowing steadily down, washing the dust from the summer grass, from the apple leaves and the late fruit still on the boughs°, what it meant to the English as a people. The rain woke in him, as nothing else had woken in him, all his feeling for England. It woke in him the misery of an exile° and the longing to be home. It was a longing deeper, at that moment, than his feelings for the girl; deeper than the mere desire for escape; deeper than the war, and the things the war had done, and the desire for the war to be over. As he stood there all the memory of rain in England washed down through his blood and steadily increased the ache of home-sickness until he was suddenly and utterly° tired of the mill, the house, the river, and the flat plain, tired of speaking and thinking another language and, above all, of the complications. He felt all the Englishness of himself washed bare to the surface, clean and clear and simple as the rain.

(H. E. Bates, *Fair stood the wind for France*)

glittering: shining
unendurably: unbearably
boughs: branches
exile: being forced to live in a foreign land
utterly: completely

Nationality

Under the British Nationality Act 1948, persons born in the United Kingdom, the Channel Islands, the Isle of Man, a ship or aircraft registered in the United Kingdom, or a territory which is still a colony, are citizens of the United Kingdom and Colonies by birth. Citizenship may also be acquired°: by descent from a father who is himself a citizen, by registration – for citizens of Commonwealth member countries or of the Irish Republic, and by naturalisation. The requirements for naturalisation include five years' residence° in the United Kingdom or Colonies, good character, a sufficient knowledge of English, and the intention to reside in the United Kingdom or a colony.

A citizen of the United Kingdom and Colonies does not forfeit° his citizenship by acquiring or possessing the nationality or citizenship of another country. Any man or woman who is a citizen is, however, at liberty to renounce° citizenship if he or she acquires the nationality or citizenship of another country.

(COI pamphlet, *The population of Britain*)

acquired: obtained
residence: living in the country
forfeit: lose
renounce: give up

NATURALISATION NOTICE

Notice is hereby given that Mounir Al-Syada of 414, Fulham Palace Road, S.W.6., is applying to the Home Secretary for naturalisation, and that any person who knows any reason why naturalisation should not be granted should send a written and signed statement of the facts to the Under-Secretary of State, Home Office (Nationality Division), Lunar House, Wellesley Road, Croydon CR9 2BY.

(*S. Kensington & Chelsea News*)

PASSPORT APPLICATIONS FORM (Pas OA)

For official use
File no. . . . .
Passport no. . .
Date of issue. . .

Please read the directions carefully before answering the questions

DIRECTIONS

1. Section D may be completed by any of the following to whom you are personally known – clergyman°, medical doctor, lawyer, bank manager, magistrate, schoolteacher, police officer, and the same person should certify° one of your photographs.
2. Please note that you are required to sign the form twice.
3. When completed, the form should be sent to the office from which it was issued, with your birth certificate and two recently taken identical° passport photographs.
4. If you were not born in Ireland and if you claim to be an Irish citizen because of the birth in Ireland of one of your parents, you should submit° the birth certificate of that parent.
5. If you became a citizen of Ireland by naturalisation or registration, particulars° should be given.

SECTION A

1. Surname (block capitals) . . . .
2. Christian or First name . . . .
3. Former name(s) (if any) . . . .
4. Single, married, or widowed . . . .
5. Occupation . . . .
6. Your date of birth (as on your birth certificate). . . . .
7. Place and country of birth. . . . .
8. Do you hold an Irish or other passport? . . . If so, it should be surrendered° with this application.
9. Home address (in full) . . . .
10. Present address . . . .
11. Height . . . .
12. Colour of eyes . . . . Colour of hair . . . .
    Shape of face . . . .
13. Approximate date of departure . . . .

14. Purpose of journey (holiday, business, permanent residence abroad) ....
15. Approximate date of return ....

SECTION C – Declaration by applicant

I, the undersigned, hereby apply for an Irish passport. I solemnly and sincerely declare that the particulars furnished° herein for the purpose of this application are true and correct in every detail, that the accompanying certificate relates to me and that the accompanying photographs are photographs of me.

Signature of applicant.......... Date......

WARNING: *A person who makes a false declaration or furnishes false information for the purpose of obtaining a passport or for the purpose of assisting another person to obtain a passport is liable to prosecution°.*

(From application for an Irish passport)

clergyman: priest
certify: sign, and state that it is a 'true likeness'
identical: exactly the same
submit: send it
particulars: details
surrendered: given up
furnished: provided
liable to prosecution: may be punished

SHOWBIZ°

According to the American Academy of Motion Picture Arts and Sciences, the ape° in the movie *King Kong* is a second-class citizen, and cannot qualify for nomination° as best actor of the year. Producer Dino de Laurentis made the enquiry and was told a definite no. They said that only human beings could qualify for the award, and that the ape was considered an 'effect' and not a 'performance'. The ape may only apply for the 'special effects' Oscar°.

(*The Australian*)

showbiz: (slang) show-business, theatre and cinema life
ape: large member of the monkey family
nomination: (literally = being named) possible selection
Oscar: most important prize in cinema

2 You can't do that here!

ban v.t. (–nn–). Formally prohibit, interdict. (OE *bannan* summon, = OHG *bannan*)

ban n. Formal or authoritative prohibition; tacit prohibition by public opinion.

forbi′d v.t. (–dd–; forba′d, or forba′de; FORBIDDEN) 1. Command (person, etc.) not to do, (person, etc.) not to go to (place), (forbid him to go, him the court); not allow (person) something; person or thing to exist or happen; *forbid him wine*; *was forbidden wine*; *wine was forbidden him*). 2. (Of circumstances, hindrance, etc.) exclude, prevent, make undesirable, (God forbid!, may it not happen!). [OE *forbēodan*, = OHG *farbiotan*].

prohibit v.t. forbid, debar, (action, thing, person's doing, person from doing); prohibited DEGREES; hence –er, –or, ns. [ME, f. L PRO (*hibēre hibit-* = *habēre* hold)].

prosecūte v.t. Follow up, pursue, (inquiry, studies); carry on (trade, pursuit); institute legal proceedings against (person) or with reference to (claim, crime, etc.), or abs. (*trespassers will be prosecuted*; *shall not prosecute*). [ME, f. L PRO (*sequi secut*-follow)].

(*The Concise Oxford Dictionary*)

[The person talking is typical of the difficult guards one often meets in front of factories, large public buildings, hospitals, building sites, etc.]

'Now look squire° why don't you push off home and forget about it I've told you before if it was up to me it would be a different story and that kind of language won't get you anywhere look it's not me that makes the rules I just work here you can write letters to who you want I'm not stopping you I understand your point of view you've come a long way but if I was to let in anyone I felt sorry for it would be more than my job's worth so why don't you run along look I don't care who you are you could be bloody Aristotle Onassis it wouldn't make no difference I'm just doing my job we've all got a job to do now don't you threaten violence on me I'm not responsible for the rules I'm just doing my job . . .'

(*Private Eye book of bores*)

squire: (old fashioned) sir

NOTICE

This Mews is private property. The parking of Cars is prohibited except by Residents in front of their own premises.

By Order
THE GROSVENOR ESTATE

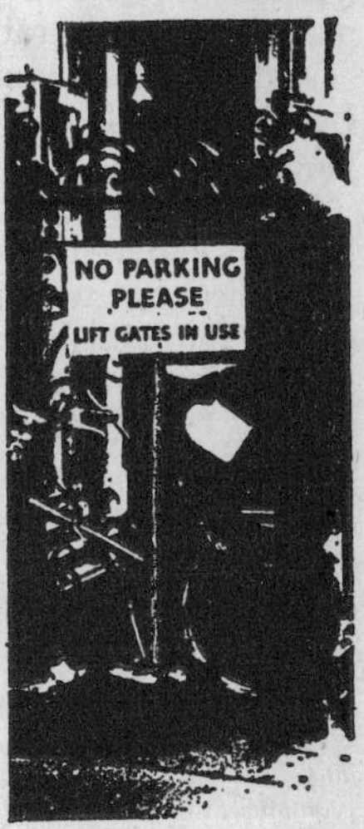

Mews: places where horses used to be kept, now turned into houses
Residents: people living in that place
premises: building

Entry into Britain

The personal baggage and belongings of all persons arriving in Britain are subject to Customs examination.

What to declare

If staying less than six months: anything which is to be sold, given away, or left in Britain and any spirits°, wines, cigars, cigarettes and tobacco in excess of° the duty-free° allowances for accompanied luggage. If staying more than six months: all articles obtained outside Britain.

Prohibited° and restricted° imports

Imports of certain goods are prohibited or restricted. They include: counterfeit° coins; addictive drugs; firearms and ammunition°; plants, and certain vegetables and fruits; radio transmitters (including 'walkie-talkies'); meat and poultry° (not fully cooked) from most countries; domestic animals (including dogs and cats); birds; and the majority of mammals (for example, rabbits, mice, monkeys and guinea pigs).

A dog or cat should not be embarked° for the voyage to Britain until the owner has been given the number of the landing licence.[1]

Birds of the parrot family (for example, budgerigars) may be freely imported into Great Britain.

Applications to import birds of the parrot family, poultry or eggs into Northern Ireland should be made to the Department of Agriculture for Northern Ireland.

1. These restrictions do not apply to the movement of cats and dogs between the Channel Islands and Britain or the Irish Republic and Britain, provided that they have not been imported from any country outside the British Isles within the preceding six months.

(COI pamphlet, Residence in Britain)

spirits: alcohol, e.g. whisky, brandy
in excess of: more than
duty-free: not taxed
prohibited: not allowed
restricted: limited
counterfeit: false
ammunition: bullets
poultry: chickens, ducks, geese, etc.
embarked: put onto a boat

When an order to stop singing is for the birds°

TORONTO: Birds are permitted to sing for only half an hour during the day and no more than 15 minutes at night. That is one of the regulations in a new by-law aimed at curbing° noise in the village of Lakefield.

Now council clerk, Earl Cuddie, the man responsible for drafting° the law, has been flooded with telephone calls from all over Canada. All ask the same question: 'How do you stop birds singing?'

Mr Cuddie sadly admits: 'I shall have to draw up a new by-law as soon as possible. The council had been complaining about the noise in the village and I guess I drafted the law in such a hurry I just didn't stop to think.'

(*Sunday Express*)

for the birds: a play on words: (1) intended for the birds; (2) no good
curbing: reducing
drafting: formulating, drawing up

On the back wall of the Hauptbahnhof in Zürich there is a notice in four languages. The English version says this:

> IT IS PROHIBITED IN THIS WAITING ROOM TO
> - remain for any length of time
> - smoke
> - consume alcohol, or
> - lie on the benches, radiators or floor
>
> PERSONS WHO HAVE CONSUMED TOO MUCH ALCOHOL, PERSONS BEHAVING INDECENTLY° AND PERSONS VIOLATING° THESE REGULATIONS ARE NOT ALLOWED IN THIS WAITING ROOM.
>
> *Swiss Federal Railways*

(Newspaper report)

indecently: improperly
violating: not obeying

Court orders pensioner° to play piano

A pensioner who shoplifted° will pay her debt to society by playing the piano.

Phyllis Mary Fishwick, aged 63, of New Cross Road, London, pleaded guilty° yesterday to stealing a bag and two pairs of tights, valued together at £16.35, from a West End store.

Sir Eric Miller, the chairman, said, 'We believe you can play the piano fairly well.' Mrs Fishwick, a divorced mother of three children, whose parents were both entertainers, replied: 'Yes, I have spoken to the probation officer° about it.'

Mrs Fishwick was ordered to do 100 hours community service work by playing the piano at an old people's home during social evenings.

(*The Times*)

pensioner: person (usually over 60), who is no longer working
shoplifted: stole from a shop
pleaded guilty: admitted she had stolen
probation officer: a person who watches over the behaviour of first-time offenders (who are on probation)

Ancient washday blues

MR ROBERT MINICAN has been banned from washing his car outside his own house because of a 129-year-old Act.

Mr Minican was banned under the 1847 Town Police Clauses Act which prohibits° the disposal of any dirt or rubbish in a public road, including the dirty water which runs off a washed car.

He said: 'I cannot remember how many years I've washed my car there. Then out of the blue° I was told by a policeman that I was committing an offence and ordered to move on. It seems ridiculous that I cannot clean my car outside my home. Any dirty water that does run off goes down the drain, so I don't see the harm.'

A police spokesman said: 'This particular Act prohibits almost anything in a public road which may cause annoyance or obstruction to other people. I cannot comment on Mr Minican's case except to say that it is an offence to wash your car on a public road.'

(*The Guardian*)

prohibits: forbids
out of the blue: (idiomatic) unexpectedly

Driving abroad

National laws. Regulations and driving habits vary from country to country. But it is sensible to assume that all countries have laws penalising° drivers who have been drinking, and that seat belts are obligatory°. Speed limits also vary, but are usually indicated at frontiers. It is wise to observe them since penalties can be severe and imposed°on the spot. So carry some cash – just in case. Note these points about some West European countries.

A *Austria.* First-aid kit and warning triangle° are compulsory°. Driving licence will be confiscated° for an alcohol offence. On mountain roads, the vehicle travelling uphill has right of way.

B *Belgium.* Traffic from the right – even from a minor road – has right of way. So have trams. If you are involved in an accident you must stay at the scene until the police allow you to leave.

F *France.* Seat belts are compulsory outside built-up areas. Traffic coming from the right invariably has right of way. If you are found to be over the alcohol limit (0.80 as in Britain) you can be imprisoned for between 10 and 30 days as well as fined.

NL *Holland.* Frontier guards can be difficult about allowing toy guns in – real ones of course are banned°. Watch out for bicycles – thousands of them. Seat belts compulsory for driver and front-seat passenger unless they are under five feet (1.6 metres) tall. Children under six must sit in the back.

I *Italy.* There is no fixed limit for the drink and drive laws, but the penalties are heavy (up to six months imprisonment). Very Italian. Translation of driving licence essential.

P *Portugal.* Beware of fast drivers on country roads. On-the-spot fines for most offences.

D *West Germany.* A red warning triangle is compulsory. Parking facing the oncoming traffic is forbidden.

YU *Yugoslavia.* Red triangle compulsory. Drivers must stop and help anybody injured in a road accident.

If the police think you have caused an accident, they may detain you first and argue about it afterwards.

(*The Sunday Times Magazine*)

penalising: punishing
obligatory: must be (worn)
imposed: put into force
triangle: see illustration
compulsory: (see obligatory) must be (carried)
confiscated: taken away
banned: forbidden

Cyclists

What to learn

- Don't carry two people on a bike
- Don't weave° in and out of traffic
- Don't ride 'no hands'
- Don't wear loose flapping clothes
- Don't hang onto other cyclists or vehicles

- Do give hand signals – especially when turning right
- Do use cycle paths where provided
- Do tell someone where you're going
- Do maintain° your bike regularly

(*The Sunday Times Magazine*)

weave: zig-zag, twist and turn
maintain: keep in working order

Take it from
Green Cross Man
KEEP LOOKING
KEEP LISTENING
WHILE YOU CROSS

H.M.S. DISCOVERY
ANTARCTIC EXPEDITION SHIP 1901/4
OPEN TO VISITORS DAILY
1300 To 1630.
ADMISSION FREE

Visitors boarding this Ship do so at their own risk. No liability will be accepted by the Ministry of Defence or their agents for Injury, Including fatal injury, loss or damage to persons or property.

liability: responsibility
fatal: resulting in death

(Sign outside shop, Hampstead)

DANGER
DEMOLITION
IN
PROGRESS

PEDESTRIANS ARE WARNED
NOT TO WALK ON ROADWAY

ROMINAR LTD.
DANGER
MEN WORKING
OVERHEAD

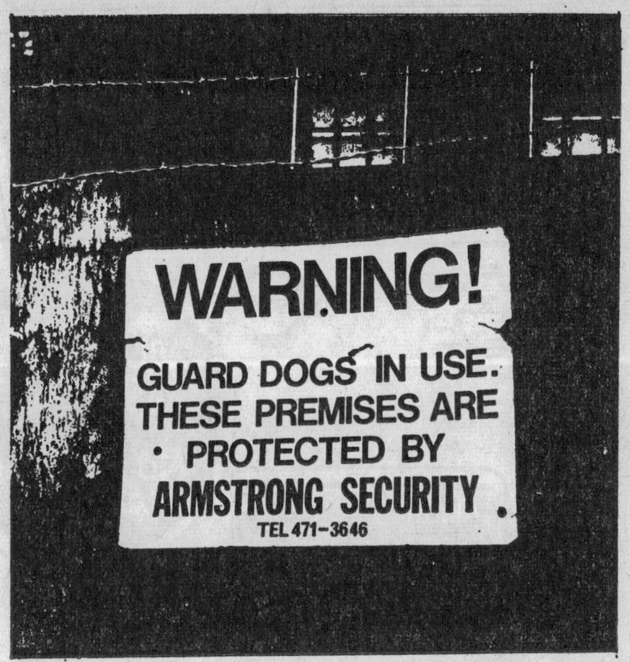

**BILL POSTERS
WILL BE
PROSECUTED**

demolition: pulling down an old building
premises: buildings
bill posters: people who put up notices on walls

conviction: being proved guilty
penalty: fine

FOLLOW THE CODE LAID OUT ON THIS PAGE AND HAVE A HAPPY BONFIRE NIGHT

NEVER FOOL WITH FIREWORKS!

firework: see illustration
code: system of rules
pets: house animals, cats, dogs, etc.
bonfire: a large fire, usually made at festivals
fool: play

Keep fireworks° injuries down

The number of people injured by fireworks has halved in the last six years, and as Guy Fawkes night° approaches one local health official hopes to keep the figures falling.

Ray Amer, health education officer for Kensington and Chelsea, said that last year 766 children received treatment after firework accidents, though there were 17% fewer serious injuries than in the previous year. Mr Amer draws attention to the firework safety code now enclosed in each box of fireworks. This advises that fireworks be kept in closed boxes, taken out only one at a time, and that the instructions be carefully read – but not by the light of a naked flame just before lighting them! They should be lit at arm's length with everyone standing well back.

Sales of fireworks are now restricted° to people of 16 or over, and letting off° a firework in a public place can draw a fine of up to £200.

(*Holburn and Finsbury Guardian*, 5.11.76)

fireworks: see illustration
Guy Fawkes (night): Guy Fawkes tried unsuccessfully to blow up the Houses of Parliament on 5 November 1605. English people remember this event every year by holding firework displays
restricted: limited
letting off: exploding

FIREWORKS
Can be dangerous

Keep them in a closed box
Follow instructions
Read instructions by torchlight
Light at arm's length
Stand back
Never go back to a firework
Never put them in your pocket
Never throw them
Keep pets indoors

(London Borough of Camden, Notice)

unattended: with no apparent owner
staff: workers

Advice to swimmers and divers in any area where shark° attacks have been recorded

The risk of shark attacks exists in any region where shark attacks on humans have been previously recorded. If entry into the water is essential, the following should be borne in mind:

1. Do not swim or dive alone at any time.
2. Do not swim at night or at any time when the light is poor.
3. Do not enter the water if you have any fresh injury (no matter how small) on your body.
4. Do not swim or dive in discoloured water.
5. The risk of attack is greatly increased in water with a temperature of 20°C or higher.
6. If you see a large shark, move away from it without delay and with as little disturbance of the water as possible.
7. To swim with a speared° fish is to invite an attack by a shark.
8. If you are not within easy reach of a boat or the shore and a shark makes an approach, you should: (*a*) try to remain calm (*b*) swim steadily towards safety, keeping the shark continuously in view (*c*) in the event of the shark attacking, take the offensive° as the shark closes in and hit it on the snout° with any hard object or with the fish.

Immediate action in the event of an attack

1. Assist the victim to safety as quickly as possible.
2. Place the victim in the head-down position to ensure a supply of blood to the brain and do everything possible to stop the bleeding.
3. Call for immediate medical assistance.
4. Do not administer° stimulants such as warm drinks or alcohol.
5. Cover the victim with a light wrap or towel, but not with heavy blankets, etc.
6. Morphine, 0.25g, should be given whether the victim is in pain or not.

(David Davies, *About sharks and shark attack*)

shark: large fish with big jaws
speared: caught (using an underwater gun)
take the offensive: attack
snout: nose
administer: give

3 Ideal job for the right person

She say 'Will you work for Jesus?'
I say 'How much Jesus pay?'
She say 'Jesus don't pay nothing.'
I say 'I won't work today.'

(Kenneth Allsop, *Hard travellin'*)

Why Britain is in Trouble

For any given task here there are more men than are needed. Strong unions° keep them there. In Fleet Street, home of some of London's biggest dailies°, it is understood that when two unions quarrel over three jobs, the argument is settled by giving each union two. That means 33 per cent overmanning, 33 per cent less productivity than could be obtained.

A reporter who has visited plants° throughout Europe has an impression that the pace of work is much slower here. Nobody tries too hard. Tea breaks do matter and are frequent. It is hard to measure intensity° of work, but Britons give a distinct impression of going at their tasks in a more leisurely° way.

But is all this so terrible? It certainly does not improve the gross national product° or output per worker. Those observant visitors, however, have noticed something else about Britain. It is a pleasant place.

Street crowds in Stockholm, Dusseldorf, Paris and New York hustle and bustle, heads down, all in a hurry. London crowds tend to amble° (except in the profitable, competitive, efficient City, the financial district). Every stranger is struck by the patient and orderly way in which Britons queue for a bus; if the saleswoman is slow and out of stock, she will likely say, 'Oh dear, what a pity,'; the rubbish collectors stop to chat and call the housewives 'Luv'. Crime rises here as in every city, but there still remains a gentle tone and temper that is unmatched in Zürich, Milan or Detroit.

In short, what is wrong with Britain may also be what is right. Having reached a tolerable° standard, Britons appear to be choosing leisure over goods.

(Adapted from an article by Bernard Nossiter in *The Washington Post*, printed in *The Guardian Weekly*)

unions: organizations of workers in the same trade or profession
dailies: newspapers
plants: factories
intensity: energy put into work
leisurely: unhurried
gross national product: the country's total industrial production in one year
amble: walk slowly
tolerable: fair, reasonable

England in the nineteenth century

In the country the average° labourer was probably not worse off in 1830 than in 1790; the average manual worker in the towns, when in employment, was possibly a little better off.

Averages°, especially for the period 1815–50, do not reveal° the condition of the lowest-paid workers or of the unemployed. As late as 1901 Rowntree's investigations at York showed that 43.4 per cent of the wage-earning class, or about a quarter of the population, lived on incomes insufficient° to meet bare physical needs. Nevertheless, the amount of misery° had diminished° as the years passed. Conditions of labour had also improved. Since this improvement was due largely to the trade unions° it was mainly in hours of work; housing conditions could not be improved by strikes°. By 1850 the textile° industries had won a ten-and-a-half-hour day and a sixty-hour week. Twelve years later the engineering industries obtained a nine-hour day. The general aim was an eight-hour day; this aim was reached between 1885 and 1900 in many industries.

(E. L. Woodward, *History of England*)

average: normal
averages: figures
reveal: show
insufficient: not enough
misery: unhappiness, poverty
diminished: decreased
trade unions: organizations of workers in the same trade or profession
strikes: decision by the workers to stop work in order to get better conditions or higher pay
textiles: cloth, material

Everything, even progress, stops for tea

THE TRADITIONAL British tea break and its abuse° are blamed in a report yesterday as being among the reasons why Britain's plant° construction is slower than abroad.

British jobs, it says, take longer than similar foreign ones, and less of the working day is spent actually working – largely because of more generous allowances for such things as tea breaks, walking and wasting time.

(*Yorkshire Post*)

abuse: wrong use, i.e. taking too much time for tea
plant: factory, power station, or similar building

*

ALF'S CUPPA°...

WHEN Alf Danks put the kettle on for his early morning cuppa yesterday, it woke the whole village.

His match for the stove caused a gas explosion at Chadsmoore in Staffordshire. Alf was only slightly burned, but his cottage was destroyed.

(*Sunday Mirror*)

cuppa: (colloquial) cup of tea

Tea breaks

Sir, – Your readers may have gained the impression from your report of our survey° of engineering construction sites – here and abroad – that our problems are mainly due to tea breaks.

This is not what the survey said. In 88 pages, references to tea breaks occupied no more than a few lines. The survey discussed at much greater length many factors° which can contribute to poor performance° including, for example, inefficient planning, design changes, delays in delivery, insecurity of employment, and wages which do not motivate° and reward effort.

J. E. Mortimer
Chairman, Mechanical and
Electrical Engineering Construction
EDC

(*The Guardian*)

survey: report
factors: reasons
performance: work
motivate: stimulate

"Delegation, sir, from the clerks and others protesting about longer bank hours."

delegation: group of representatives

Industrial Disputes°

BUTCHERS Two hundred workers of the A. J. Bush chain of butcher shops in Sydney are continuing a strike° which has lasted two weeks.

The strikers want wage increases of $23 to $26 a week to bring them to parity° with meatworkers employed in supermarkets.

FUNERALS A strike by gravediggers and crematorium° workers is likely to end tomorrow when the Funeral and Allied Employees' Association will recommend a return to work.

GOVERNMENT PRINTERS Striking printers employed at the Government Printing Office will meet today to discuss the progress in negotiations° during their six-day strike. The 600 men are striking in support of a man threatened with dismissal for alleged° inefficiency°.

(*Sydney Morning Herald*)

disputes: disagreements
strike: decision by all or most workers to stop work in order to get better working conditions or higher pay
parity: equal level
crematorium: place where bodies are burnt
negotiations: discussions
alleged: claimed, supposed
inefficiency: not working properly

'Meaningless' reason given for sacking°

A firm which sacked a man for 'lack of urgency'° has been told it must be more specific°.

An Industrial Tribunal chairman last Thursday described the reason as 'meaningless' and told the firm to provide examples before the case was decided.

Mr Horace Hopkins worked for Segal Textiles Ltd for six years and then, he claims, he was unfairly sacked.

The chairman of the Tribunal said that Mr Hopkins was entitled° to know exactly what was alleged° against him. Merely to say 'lack of urgency' was meaningless. The company had to give particulars of occasions when Mr Hopkins had failed to carry out his duties.

(*Hampstead and Highgate Express*)

sacking: (colloquial) being sent away from one's job
(lack of) urgency: (no sense of the need for) immediate action
specific: detailed
entitled: had the right
alleged: stated

(Punch)

"Couldn't you just try to do it with a little more energy?"

Dismissed? Redundant°? Job hunting?

If you were told tomorrow by your employer that he no longer needed your services and that you could leave in so many weeks' time, would you know what to do? What your rights were? How much money you should get? How to cope° while unemployed and the best way of setting about getting yourself another job?

A new Consumer Publication has just been produced to help you in such a situation. It tells you first about the legal aspects of dismissal, and then goes on to suggest how you should get down to the business of job hunting – organising yourself, writing letters of application, preparing for interviews and making the best of yourself when interviewed. Finally, the book discusses the decisions about what job to accept. Claiming unemployment benefit is explained, and other state help while looking for a job. *Dismissal, redundancy and job hunting* costs £1.50 and can be ordered on the form in this month's *Which?*

(*Which?*)

redundant: forced to leave your job because there is not enough work
cope: manage

You're clever. And personable. But when you go for a job...

there's this terrible problem. The man across the desk asks you a question. You know the answer but you don't reply. *Because you can't hear a word he's saying.*

Every casual° meeting that most of us take for granted° can be an enormous problem to the deaf. Communicating with people at work. Ordering a meal in a restaurant. Meeting the opposite sex.

The RNID tries to help deaf people. We run a residential school, a hostel and training centre, and homes for the elderly. If you can hear, will you be thankful? And help someone less fortunate.

Please send your donation to
Royal National Institute for the Deaf
Room 11, Freepost, Glasgow G37BR

(Advertisement)

personable: attractive
casual: chance, everyday
take for granted: accept without thinking

Jobs

ANIMAL-LOVER to walk two small dogs in private gardens for 20 minutes during period 7.30–8.15 a.m. School child considered. 50p per day.
(*Hampstead Express*)

PART-TIME early morning delivery person to deliver papers to homes six days a week. Must have a reliable vehicle and be an early riser.
(*Toronto Globe & Mail*)

CLEANER female, weekend only, 8 a.m.–12 midday. Must speak English.
(*Sydney Morning Herald*)

WORK

BUTCHER. Immediate start. Ferndale Butchery. Riverwood.
DISHWASHER required for City Restaurant. Experience essential.
(*Sydney Morning Herald*)

BAR STEWARDESS. Experienced girl required for casual position, weekend/evening work. Phone Mr Walpole 699 4156.

YOUNG DRUMMER WANTED. Must look great, play great, for exciting new rock band.
(*Melody Maker*)

EXPERIENCED MECHANIC required for overland expeditions to Africa. Telephone Long Haul Expeditions 440 1582.
(*Australasian Express*, London)

SITUATIONS

SALES REPRESENTATIVE. A quality company, market leaders° in the medical supply area, are seeking an individual with potential° to move up quickly within their organization. A degree is essential as well as a few years of sales experience. $18,000+ car.
(*Toronto Globe & Mail*)

ASSISTANT CONTROLLER. $13,000. Excellent opportunity to join the staff of a major hotel. Several years hotel accounting experience is required. Ability to supervise° a large staff required.
(*Toronto Globe & Mail*)

SITUATIONS. *Au Pair* experts have a fantastic selection of girls available immediately. Most nationalities.
(*Hampstead & Highgate Express*)

Positions vacant

Top Chef° Required
Also Manager for elegant large restaurant PERTH
Write for details

ENGINEER/TECHNICAL OFFICER – ITALIAN-SPEAKING A position exists for a qualified Engineer to undertake translation of Technical Documents from Italian into English.
Salary will be commensurate° with qualifications and experience. Enquiries initially to: Staff Officer, Amalgamated Wireless (Australasia).

(*The Australian*)

APPOINTMENTS

Social Work Advisers – £5,990–£8,060
There are three vacancies for professionally qualified and experienced social workers in the social work services group. Some travel is involved.
Candidates, preferably aged at least 30, must hold a university qualification in applied social studies and have sound relevant° experience at senior level.

(*The Observer*)

market leaders: an important company
potential: ability
supervise: manage
chef: cook
commensurate: in proportion to
relevant: suitable

The short list°

Only a little thought is needed to convince us that the perfect advertisement should attract only one reply and that from the right man. Let us begin with an extreme example:

Wanted: Acrobat° capable of crossing a wire 63 metres above raging furnace°. Twice nightly, 3 times on Saturday. Salary offered, £25 per week, No pension and no compensation° in the event of injury. Apply in person at Wildcat Circus between the hours of 9 a.m. and 10 a.m.

The wording of this may not be perfect but the *aim* should be so to balance the inducement° in salary against the possible risks involved that only a single applicant will appear. It is needless to insist that applicants should be physically fit, sober°, and free from fits of dizziness°. They know that. It is just as needless to say that those nervous of heights need not apply. They won't. The skill of the advertiser consists in adjusting° the salary to the danger. An offer of £1,000 per week might produce a dozen applicants. An offer of £15 might produce none. Somewhere between those two figures lies the exact sum, the minimum figure to attract anyone actually capable of doing the job.

(C. Northcote Parkinson, *Parkinson's law*)

the short list: the best 3–5 of the applicants for a job
acrobat: usually works in a circus; performs daring acts with his body
furnace: fire
compensation: payment for injuries in accidents
inducement: attraction
sober: one who is not under the influence of drink
dizziness: feeling of turning in the head
adjusting: fitting

A team of surgeons° worked yesterday to sew back a circus juggler's° right thumb which was bitten off by a zebra° in Sydney, Australia. The zebra is as well as can be expected; surgeons say it will be some time before they know if their operation was successful.

(*Yorkshire Post*)

surgeons: doctors
juggler: man who can keep many objects moving in the air at the same time
zebra: animal the size of a small horse, with black and white stripes

---

A Canner°

A canner exceedingly canny°,
One morning remarked to his Granny,
'A canner can can
Anything that he can,
But a canner can't can a can, can he?'

(Traditional American)

canner: person who works in a factory, putting food or drink into tins
canny: clever

*

NO RUNNING IN THE CANNERY

(Sign in a Yorkshire sausage factory)

Unwanted mothers

When will employers learn to treat job applicants who happen to be mothers of young children as they would treat other applicants°?

I wonder how many mothers, like myself, have faced an interviewer who seemed more concerned with the applicants' private life than with their ability to do the job. The job that I applied for involved evening work; my interviewer was not nosy° enough to ask who would care for my child while I worked, but he had the audacity° to ask: 'Won't your husband mind looking after him?' I doubt if any husbands who go for job interviews are asked if their wives mind looking after the children five days a week while they work; yet intelligent women must put up with this insane° questioning.

My private life has nothing to do with the interviewer. Even if it had, a child has two parents and I believe that they should share in her or his upbringing. Only the totally inadequate mother would apply for a job without being confident that her children wouldn't suffer by it.

It's hard enough in this country for parents to make acceptable arrangements for their children while they work, so if a young mother can manage to work a few hours a week, why not give her credit for it? Mothers like myself who have undergone a lengthy education at the taxpayer's expense should not be prevented from using that education productively by narrow-minded employers.

(Jennifer Harvey, *The Sunday Times*)

applicants: people asking (applying) for jobs
nosy: wanting to know too many personal details
audacity: nerve, cheek
inane: stupid

Plenty of work for ratcatchers

THE HAGUE: Six hundred people have applied for the job of ratcatcher in the eastern province of Drenthe. The applicants are mostly farmers wanting to sell up° and unemployed office workers. The wage? £80 a week. But even in these times of rising unemployment it is considered a safe job. For some 70,000 rats are caught each year.

(*Sunday Express*)

sell up: leave their farms

The ratcatcher

'Now listen. I'll tell you.' The ratman advanced a step closer. 'You works° on the understanding that a rat is a gnawin'° animal, see. Rats *gnaws*. Anythin' you give them, don't matter what it is, anythin' new they never seen before. And what do they do? They *gnaws* it. So now! There you are! You get a sewer° job on your hands. And what do you do?'

His voice had the soft throaty sound of a croaking frog. The accent was similar to Claud's, the broad soft accent of the Buckinghamshire countryside.

'All you do is you go down the sewer and you take along some ordinary paper bags, just ordinary brown paper bags, and these bags is filled with Plaster of Paris powder°. Nothin' else. Then you suspend the bags from the roof of the sewer so they hang down not quite touchin' the water. See? Not quite touchin', and just high enough so a rat can reach them.'

Claud was listening carefully.

'There you are, y'see. Old rat comes swimmin' along the sewer and sees the bag. He stops. He takes a sniff at it and it don't smell so bad anyway. So what's he do then?'

'He gnaws it,' Claud cried, delighted.

'There? That's it! That's exactly it! He starts *gnawin'* away at the bag and the bag breaks and the old rat gets a mouthful of powder for his pains.'

'Well?'

'That does him.'

'What? Kills him?'

'Yep. Kills him stoney°.'

'Plaster of Paris ain't poisonous, you know.'

'Ah! There you are! That's exactly where you're wrong, see. This powder swells°. When you wet it, it swells. Gets into the rat's tubes and swells right up and kills him quicker than anythin' in the world.'

'*No!*'

'That's where you've got to know rats.'

The ratman's face glowed with a stealthy° pride, and he rubbed his stringy fingers together, holding the hands up close to his face. Claud watched him, fascinated.

'Now – where's them rats? Let's take a look at them *rraats*.'

(Roald Dahl, The ratcatcher, from *Someone like you*)

(you) works: (incorrect) work; the ratcatcher does not speak 'correct' English
gnawin': gnawing – biting with the front teeth
sewer: drain; all cities have sewers to take away dirty water
Plaster of Paris powder: powder which hardens with water, used e.g. for holding broken arms in place
stoney: (dialect) stone dead
swells: gets bigger, like bread in the oven
stealthy: secret

One night, recently, a taxi driver in New York began grumbling° to me, his passenger, about what a 'lousy'° business hacking° is. He longed to get a job 'selling' or something, but continued, 'Who in hell will take a hackie?' Previously, he indicated, he had held a variety of jobs including being a photographer's assistant and a part-time dancing instructor. His name, I noted, indicated that he was an Italian American. He said that as a hackie he was lucky to average $75 a week. I mentioned that I had heard that a nearby industrial plant° paid workmen more than $100, and inquired if he had thought of trying that.

He recoiled° in horror and almost swung us off the road. I had insulted him. He said he wouldn't consider such work. Why?

'You get your hands dirty. I don't like to get my hands dirty.'

'What does your father do?'

(Shame in voice). 'Oh, he's just a labouring man. A stone mason°.'

'I hear masons are making good money these days.'

'Yeah. He's got it fine now, if you can take that sort of thing. Makes $150 a week, easy. Has short days, long vacations. Even has an assistant. Still, I wouldn't want any part of it. He puts on dirty clothes.' At this, the hackie made a face.

(Vance Packard, *The status seekers*)

grumbling: complaining
lousy: dreadful, useless
hacking: being a taxi driver (hackie)
plant: factory
recoiled: drew back
mason: cutter

Meetings

Nearly all managers spend a large proportion of their time in meetings (just as their secretaries say).

Simple logic dictates° that the more people attend a meeting the less effectively the time of its average member is used. If four people meet for an hour and talk for an equal amount of time (an unlikely story), each is active for a quarter of an hour and passive for three quarters. If eight people meet for the same length of time, the active–passive ratio° declines from 1:3 to 1:7.

In practice, the time taken expands to accommodate° the numbers present, rather than the subject matter. So eight managers take two hours where four take one hour, and so on. It hardly matters that the meeting is formally called a committee or that some of those attending are asleep (or wish they were). The principle is always the same – the more people there are present, the more managerial time is wasted.

(Robert Heller, *The naked manager*)

simple logic dictates: reason clearly proves
ratio: (mathematical) relation
accommodate: suit

The famous pianist Arthur Rubinstein was asked to examine students at the Academy of Music in Paris.

The marks they could be given ranged from 0–20.

It was noticed during the exam that Rubinstein gave each student either 0 or 20.

When he was asked why, he said: 'Well, either they can play the piano, or they can't!'

4 Why don't things fall off?

THE WEATHER

Wet in north,
fog in south

Pressure will remain low over southern Britain with a cold easterly airstream across northern areas.

London, SE, central, S, E England, East Anglia, Midlands, Wales: Dull, fog which may be persistent°. Mostly dry. Wind variable light. Maximum temperature 6 °C.

Outlook°: Cold in the north, with sleet° or snow at times; rather cold in the south with rain at times.

(*The Guardian*, 21.12.76)

Today's Weather

Sydney: A warm to hot day with sunny periods. Afternoon coastal seabreezes°, fresh at times, seas slight° but occasionally choppy°. Temperature range: 19 to 28 °C.

Brisbane: Fine. Sultry°. Light winds and an afternoon seabreeze. Temperature range: 22 to 33 °C.

Darwin: A few afternoon and over-night thunderstorms. Light to moderate northwest winds. Temperature range: 26 to 33 °C.

(*The Australian*, 30.12.76)

WEATHER REPORT

Toronto: A few flurries° and milder with moderate southerly winds. High near freezing.

North Bay: Occasional snow and not as cold. Moderate southerly winds. High. −10 to −8.

Ottawa, Montreal: Sunny this morning, increasing cloudiness later. High −10 to −8 except near −12 in the Laurentians.

Long-range outlook: Northern Ontario – windy and cold with snow flurries tomorrow. Lows −18 to −22. Highs −12 to −8.

(*Toronto Globe & Mail*, 14.12.76)

persistent: lasting
outlook: weather likely in the next few days
sleet: icy rain
seabreezes: light winds from the sea
slight: fairly calm
choppy: a little rough
sultry: hot, without wind
flurries: snowstorms

THIS IS THE GATE OF HEAVEN
ENTER YE ALL BY THIS DOOR

This door is kept locked because of the draught

Notice at Cumberland church

ye: (old English) you
draught: air current

If the earth is round . . .

'But if the earth is round, sir, why don't things fall off it? Why don't people and things and the seas fall off it?'

'Because, my dear Arendse, it has a gravitational pull° which prevents all these things happening.'

'Then, sir, will you please explain this pull thing to us?'

'Yes, sir.'

'Please . . .'

'Do you, Arendse, and all the others, do you realise that there is a strict set scheme for each class? Certain things are taught in standard one, certain things in standard two, and so on. Gravity and science are things you shouldn't know anything about till next year.'

'But sir . . .'

'Well?'

'That means that till next year we've just got to accept your word about everything you say about the earth. And for a year we'll go on wanting to know how things stick to the earth if it is round.'

'And you know Mr Visser° told us always to ask if things didn't seem very clear to us.'

'All right! Sit down, Flora, and you, Arendse. Mr Visser's specials! . . . Before I go on to gravity, Peter's been snapping his fingers. What is it you want to know, Peter?'

'When you talked about how to prove the earth is round, sir, you said the curve° of the land was sure proof. But the land is full of hills and valleys; so how can one see this curve? And none of us have been to sea, so we don't know whether it does curve. So you see, sir, if you answer Arendse's question before proving the earth is round it will be hard to believe in this pull, because you won't need it on a flat earth.'

'You are the original flat-earthers! Now listen! . . .

(Peter Abrahams, *The green years*)

gravitational pull: force attracting things to the centre of the earth
Mr Visser: another teacher
curve: line which bends, i.e. the horizon

First, then, a few general remarks about the Sun. It is the nearest of the stars – a hot self-luminous° globe. Though only a star of moderate size, the Sun is enormously greater than the Earth and the other planets. It contains about 1,000 times as much material as Jupiter, the largest planet, and over 300,000 times as much as the Earth. Its gravitational° attraction controls the motions of the planets, and its rays supply the energy that maintains nearly every form of activity on the surface of the Earth.

(Fred Hoyle, *The nature of the Universe*)

self-luminous: providing its own light
gravitational: the power with which the Sun and Moon 'pull' the Earth

---

The restless tides°

Since Greek and Roman times men have known that the rhythm of the tides was somehow related to the apparent motion of the Moon and the Sun, but it was not until Newton's time that we were given a rational° explanation of this link. In his *Principia*, published in 1687, Newton showed that the tides are one of the consequences of the law of gravitation. Every particle° of matter on the Earth is attracted by the Moon, and the force of attraction is directed towards the Moon's centre; also, the farther away from the Moon's centre the particle is, the weaker the attracting force. So the force varies° slightly in both direction and strength. It is this variation in the attracting force that causes the ocean waters to move backwards and forwards and so produce the tides. As we might expect, the tidal forces tend to cause the water on the side of the Earth facing the Moon to be heaped up. Because the ocean waters on the far side of the Earth (most distant from the Moon) are the least affected by the Moon's gravitational attraction, they tend, in a sense, to be left behind.

We know that the Sun also has an effect on the tides. It may seem surprising that this effect is not greater, since the Sun is nearly 25 million times more massive° than the Moon. But mass is not the only key to the explanation. The Sun's greater distance from us is the dominating° fact, with the result that its ability to raise tides on Earth is less than half that of the Moon.

(G. Deacon, *Oceans*)

tides: movements of the sea four times a day, twice towards the shore (high tide) and twice away (low tide)
rational: scientific
particle: tiny piece
varies: changes
(more) massive: bigger in body and volume
dominating: most important

EACH THING that goes away returns and nothing in the end is lost. The great friend throws all things apart and brings all things together again. This is the way everything goes and turns round. That is how all living things come back after long absences, and in the whole great world all things are living things. All that goes returns. He will return.

How can I not know it when all my years I have watched the sun go down times unending toward the night only to come again from the dawn the opposite way? Too true, it is so long since I last saw the sun, going or coming. But my skin continues to tell the heat from the cold, and I know it is I who have changed, not the changing circle of the world itself. And yet even here things have come about° lately to put me into more fearful doubts than my tired soul can hold. Have two nights passed? Or is it two whole weeks that have passed me by?

(Ayi Kwei Armah, *Fragments*)

come about: happened

You are never dedicated° to something you have complete confidence in. No one is fanatically° shouting that the sun is going to rise tomorrow. They *know* it's going to rise tomorrow. When people are fanatically dedicated to political or religious faiths or any other kinds of dogmas° or goals, it's always because these dogmas or goals are in doubt.

(Robert Pirsig, *Zen and the art of motorcycle maintenance*)

dedicated: strongly attached, deeply involved in
fanatically: with blind certainty
dogmas: absolute theories, beliefs or principles

The beautiful eyes of Polaroid

See what happens in Polaroid sunglasses.

We went around the world for these sunglasses. From Italy to England, France, South Africa and Australia. (And you have the largest range to choose from.)

And yet they all have Polaroid's famous lenses that can filter out° up to 99 % of that glare° that bounces into your eyes off the sand and water.

Polaroid sunglasses. The view is fantastic from either side.

Nobody knows the sun better than Polaroid

(Advertisement)

filter out: remove
glare: strong light

We are all convinced that the sun will rise tomorrow. Why? Is this belief a mere° blind outcome° of past experience, or can it be justified as a reasonable belief?

It is obvious that if we are asked why we believe that the sun will rise tomorrow we shall naturally answer, 'Because it always has risen every day'. We have a firm belief that it will rise in the future, because it has risen in the past. If we are challenged° as to why we believe that it will continue to rise as before, we may appeal to the laws of motion°: the earth, we shall say, is a freely rotating° body, and such bodies do not cease° to rotate unless something interferes from outside, and there is nothing outside to intefere with the earth between now and tomorrow. Of course, it might be doubted whether we are quite certain that there is nothing outside to interfere, but this is not the interesting doubt. The interesting doubt is whether the laws of motion will remain in operation until tomorrow.

The *only* reason for believing that the laws of motion will remain in operation is that they have operated up till now, so far as our knowledge of the past enables us to judge. But it becomes plain that we have no ground whatever for expecting the sun to rise tomorrow, or for expecting the bread we shall eat at our next meal not to poison us. All such expectations are only *probable*.

(Bertrand Russell, *The problems of philosophy*)

mere: just
outcome: result
challenged: asked (to prove our belief)
motion: movement of solid bodies
rotating: turning round on itself
cease: stop

'IT'

WHO or what created the universe?

WHO or what installed° the stars in outer space?

WHO or what controls the 'lever' in space and amuses himself by making stars collide°, suns explode and whole galaxies° crash into one another?

WHO or what 'breathed the breath of life' into the first form of life?

WHO or what wanted intelligent life to come into being, wanted us to become the way we are?

IF everything that is° was created by the one and only God, then that God must be righteous, omnipotent° and good, for everything is created according to his will.

WHY does this almighty God let wars take place, let blood and tears flow?

IF this God wants all men to 'serve' him, as the religions put it, why does he allow on a single planet 20,000 religions and sects who carry on bloody conflicts° with each other in his name?

HOW can two enemies at war be blessed for victory in the name of this God, who, religions say, was once a man and so must understand men in happiness and sorrow? Ought not the omniscient° God to confer His blessing only on° the party which is actually fighting in His name?

HOW can a wise and good God allow the rich to get richer and the poor poorer, when they are all His children?

WHAT meaning has this one God decreed° for intelligent life?

(Erich von Däniken, *The gold of the gods*)

installed: set
collide: hit (each other)
galaxies: groups of stars
is: exists
omnipotent: all-powerful
conflicts: fights, battles
omniscient: all knowing
confer . . . on: give . . . to
decreed: laid down, determined

The Maya

What most remarkably distinguished the civilization of the Maya from all others was an obsession° with the passage of time. Maya intellectual life was almost entirely devoted° to the problem of measuring its flow.

To the Maya, each day was a deity°, who carried the weight of time on his back. Time was a never-ending procession of day gods, night gods, week gods, month gods, and year gods moving from the darkness of the past into the darkness of the future.

The Maya calendar consisted of two separate counts, one a solar° year, the other mainly ceremonial°. The solar year, called the *tun*, was comprised of 365 days; the ceremonial year was only 260 days long.

To measure the passage of time, the Maya studied the cycles° of the sun and the moon, and of the planet Venus, although they were unaware of the true significance of what they observed. To them the earth was flat, and the sun and the stars moved around it. But they noted the recurrent° cycles so closely that they were able to make remarkably accurate records of them.

(L. Cottrell, *Lost worlds*)

obsession: deep, powerful interest
devoted: given to
deity: god
solar: sun
ceremonial: concerned with holidays and feasts
cycles: regular movements
recurrent: occurring at repeated intervals

The Chair

A funny thing about a Chair:
You hardly ever think it's *there*.
To know a Chair is really it,
You sometimes have to go and sit.

(Theodore Roethke)

*

The Ceiling

Suppose the Ceiling went Outside
And then caught Cold and Up° and Died?
The only Thing we'd have for Proof
That he was Gone, would be the Roof;
I think it would be Most Revealing°
To find out how the Ceiling's Feeling.

(Theodore Roethke)

up: went
revealing: interesting

Why we need our heads examined

What emerges clearly from a conversation with Dr Blakemore is his strong belief that brain research involves far more than the investigation of the nervous system° by laboratory workers. Consciousness, he insists, is fundamentally° social; we understand another person's state of mind through his behaviour. Sociology is, in the end, brain research, for the brain is the instrument which has shaped our behaviour and our society.

He describes an experiment which took place on the Japanese island of Koshima. The researchers had been spreading wheat on the beach for the monkeys they were studying. Picking it up grain by grain was a slow business. But Imo, a 'genius' among monkeys, picked up handfuls of the stuff and flung° it into the sea; the sand sank and she gathered the grains from the surface. Within a few years this skill had been learned by all but the very oldest and youngest. In the same way humans share and exploit° the ideas of their most gifted individuals, and this leads to what he describes as the 'collective mind' – a communal pool of invention and discovery.

(The Reith Lectures 1976, from *Radio Times North*)

nervous system: system of nerves in the human body
fundamentally: basically
flung: threw
exploit: make use of

The most striking example of value rigidity° I can think of is the old south Indian Monkey Trap, which depends on value rigidity for its effectiveness. The trap consists of a hollowed-out coconut° chained to a stake. The coconut has some rice inside which can be grabbed through a small hole. The hole is big enough so that the monkey's hand can go in, but too small for his fist with rice in it to come out. The monkey reaches in and is suddenly trapped – by nothing more than his own value rigidity. He can't revalue the rice. He cannot see that freedom without rice is more valuable than capture with it. The villagers are coming to get him and take him away. They're coming closer . . . closer! . . . now! What general advice – not specific advice – but what *general* advice would you give the poor monkey in circumstances like this?

(Robert Pirsig, *Zen and the art of motorcycle maintenance*)

value rigidity: being unable to change your ideas
coconut: large nut, almost as big as a man's head, with white 'meat' and milk inside; grows on palm trees

The reality of differences

One may throw doubt on the reality of difference between a bearded and a clean-shaven man by first asking whether a man with one hair on his chin has a beard. The answer is clearly 'No'. Then one may ask whether with two hairs on his chin a man has a beard. Again the answer must be 'No'. So again with three, four, etc. At no point can the other person say 'Yes', for if he has answered 'No' for, let us say, 29 hairs, and 'Yes' for 30, it is easy to pour scorn on° the suggestion that the difference between 29 and 30 hairs is the difference between not having and having a beard. Yet by this process of adding one hair at a time we can reach a number of hairs which would undoubtedly make up a beard. The trouble is that the difference between a beard and no beard is like the difference between black and white, a difference between two extremes that have no sharp dividing line between them.

A similar error° lay at the back of the mind of the man who loaded his camel one straw at a time, hoping that the additional weight of a single straw would never be enough to break the camel's back. When at length the camel's back did break, he thought it was caused by the extra weight of the last straw. He supposed that because there was no sharp line between a moderate° load and a severe over-load, there was therefore no difference between them. This is a mistake which no reasonable person would make.

We do, however, frequently hear an argument against the distinction between a proletarian° and a capitalist which begins: 'When does a man become a capitalist? If a working man has £200 in the bank, is he a capitalist?' This is the argument of the beard. The truth is that the difference between those who own capital and those who do not is one of the most important of the social differences between men, although there is a continuous variation° between those who own nothing and those who own a great deal. It is equally wrong to suppose that there is a sharp dividing line between these classes and to suppose that there is no difference between them. The justification° for using the terms 'capitalist' and 'proletarian' is the same as the justification for using the words 'white' and 'black', and the use of the words is open to precisely the same dangers of creating sharply distinct classes where none in fact exist. This danger, however, is not to be dealt with° by denying the reality of the difference.

(Robert Thouless, *Straight and crooked thinking*)

pour scorn on: (idiomatic) make fun of, consider as senseless
error: mistake
moderate: reasonable, normal
proletarian: political term for a member of the true working class
variation: difference
justification: reason, explanation
(to be) dealt with: removed

'It's the last straw that breaks the camel's back'
(Popular saying)

A person who is under great strain°, and has been forced to put up with many problems and difficulties, will often give up or 'break' for an apparently small matter. Whatever the reason may be, it is called 'the last straw'. The person who breaks down or gives up will often be heard to say afterwards: 'that was the last straw!'

strain: fatigue, pressure

An elderly man who lived alone took his dinner each night in the same restaurant at the same table.

One night, after he had paid his bill and put on his hat, he walked up a wall, across the ceiling, down another wall, and out of the door.

'That's odd,' the waiter said. 'Usually he says goodnight.'

(A. Schwartz, *Witcracks*)

Did 'weeping' plant know her husband would die?

In the 'Reader's own story' section, Arene Senior, says she never liked lilies° because they remind her of passings°.

'My friend, Phyllis, gave me one she had always loved. I took it home and carefully tended° it. For two weeks the plant flourished°. Then suddenly it began giving off a sickly smell. I recognised it instantly. It was the unmistakeable smell of a sick room.

I sniffed around and found to my amazement that it was coming from the plant. Every five minutes or so it produced a small drop of water. The lily seemed to be crying.

For weeks Mrs Senior moved the plant from room to room. Whether it was in the shade or light, *'the strange smell and tears poured from it'*.

Two months later, Mrs Senior heard that her friend Phyllis had passed. *' The very morning I received the news, the lily stopped crying. The smell of illness vanished.'*

Two years ago her husband Robert, became ill. *'He recovered sufficiently to do small jobs around the house. I suggested he look after some of our indoor plants. One was a beautiful plant with pink flowers, which Robert cut back to encourage it to flower.'*

Several months later, Mrs Senior *'with dawning° fear saw this superb, healthy plant shedding tears° The crying continued day after day. I felt that only a tragedy would halt the tears. I was afraid to guess what.'*

Her husband had a heart attack; he died before the ambulance reached the hospital.

'Later, back home, I glanced at our plant. Through my tears I could see that it had stopped crying. I'm not saying the plant knew of Robert's death – just that I can't think of any other explanation.'

(*Psychic News*)

lilies: flowers, often growing on or near water
passings: death
tended: looked after
flourished: grew well
dawning: growing
shedding tears: crying

Telepathy

In all probability man has always believed that thoughts could sometimes be transmitted° from one mind to another mind *directly* and not through the usual channels of the special senses. This belief is as widespread as it is ancient°. Telepathy, as this direct transmission of thought has been called, may take place in a variety of ways, and under many different conditions. Sometimes the *recipient*° of the message has been widely awake, sometimes he has been in a drowsy° condition, and sometimes he has received the message in the form of a dream. So also have the circumstances of the *sender* of the message differed. Frequently he has been in a highly critical situation, so that the message has been accepted by the recipient as a warning of his death, but on other occasions nothing of any consequence° is happening to either of them. Telepathy may therefore take place under so many different conditions that it is likely to be occurring sometimes without our being aware of the fact.

(Kenneth Walker, *The unconscious mind*)

transmitted: sent
ancient: old
recipient: person who receives
drowsy: half asleep
consequence: importance

5 The message

Legal, decent, honest, etc. . .

For some time – no doubt like others – I have been aware of a big advertising campaign° telling me to write to the ASA (Advertising Standards Authority) if I saw an ad° that struck me as not 'Legal, decent, honest, or truthful'.

This body is attempting to do nothing less than control all advertising in the Press, in the cinema, on posters, or sent through the post. There are 37 to 40 million such ads every year.

ASA's main business is the meaning of words. There are constant battles with the advertisers about usage. What does 'unique' mean – a favourite ad-man's word? In the view of ASA's Director, Peter Thomson, the word has now become so corrupted° that it has lost any meaning at all in an advertising context. The word 'only', by contrast, still has a precise meaning, so that an advertiser who says that a product is obtainable 'only' at his shop must be able to prove it.

Words that cause constant trouble are 'new', 'tonic', 'fresh' and 'natural'. Tate and Lyle° make the following statement: 'Sugar is pure, natural energy'. True or false? (The ASA held it was true).

All ads should be decent, says the very first article of the British Code of Advertising Practice, the ASA's bible. Are bare breasts decent? Well, they seem to be becoming more acceptable to the public, so they are all right in shower advertisements but perhaps not all right in ads for taps. A bacardi rum advertisement showed a couple on a raft° with a rum bottle. The ASA decided that this contravened° Rule 2.10 which says that 'advertisements should neither claim nor suggest that any drink can contribute° towards sexual success'.

The ASA's most awkward problem, though, is cigarette smoking. The Government is in two minds: while the Department of Health thinks that all cigarette advertisements are immoral, the Treasury° is mainly concerned with the continuation of its vast tobacco revenues°. The result is the cigarette code, introduced by the ASA last March. 'In advertisements showing persons smoking, their faces should not express ecstatic° or unrealistic enjoyment of the cigarette'. The rule means it is thought, that the smoker can be smiling, but not smiling too much.

(Michael Davie, *Observer Review*)

campaign: publicity drive
ad: advertisement
corrupted: wrongly used
Tate and Lyle: sugar manufacturers
raft: a flat boat (like the Kon-Tiki)
contravened: broke, went against
contribute: help
Treasury: Government department that receives taxes
revenues: money from taxes
ecstatic: extremely joyful

Bishop raps° sexy ads

The Bishop of Bristol lashed out° last night at advertising men for appealing to the seven deadly sins. In a New Year message, the Bishop said: 'The roads to sexual success are unbelievably numerous, with chocolates, cigarettes and after-shave lotion to mention but a few.'

(*Daily Mirror*)

raps: criticizes
lashed out (at): attacked

Letters to the editor must be signed by and bear the address of the writer. Names are withheld° only in special cases. The *Sun* may edit letters for brevity°, clarity°, legality° or taste.

(*Vancouver Sun*)

withheld: not printed
brevity: shortness
clarity: clearness
legality: keeping to the law

General conditions of acceptance

The Guardian subscribes° to the Code of Advertising Practice.

The Guardian does not guarantee the insertion° of any particular advertisement on a specified date, or at all, although every effort will be made to meet the wishes of the advertiser.

The Guardian reserves the right to edit or delete° any objectionable° wording, and to reject any advertisement.

Readers are advised to take professional advice before answering advertisements inviting investment of capital°.

(*The Guardian*)

subscribes (to): supports
insertion: publication
delete: remove
objectionable: unpleasant
investment of capital: putting money into e.g. a business

NOTICE TO ADVERTISERS

Trade Descriptions Act 1968

Advertisements will only be accepted on the understanding that descriptions relating to goods are accurate and in no way contravene° the provisions of the Trade Descriptions Act 1968.

(*Yorkshire Post*)

contravene: go against

Social communication

We are daily confronted° with industry's need and use of communication. We are all aware of the fact that this is the most popular aspect of advertising.

The heading 'Social Communication' makes it clear how this aspect of advertising differs from the information and persuasion to promote° the sale of products and services. How closely one is linked to the other is exemplified° by a case in Germany: – Public telephone boxes were being vandalized°, and the Lintas agency was asked to start a campaign° to protect them. The simple but effective use of well-designed stickers saying that in an emergency° telephones can save a life produced the desired result and helped to reduce the annual° repair costs, which were previously 15 million DM.

In this particular case, advertising was used as a means° of convincing others about ideas, opinions and behaviour. Advertising, when used in this way, does not only make a social problem more apparent, but also communicates the views and opinions of governments, associations and organizations.

(Catalogue of exhibition 'Social Communication' International Advertising Association, London)

confronted: faced
promote: encourage
exemplified: shown
vandalized: destroyed
emergency: urgent case
annual: yearly
means: way

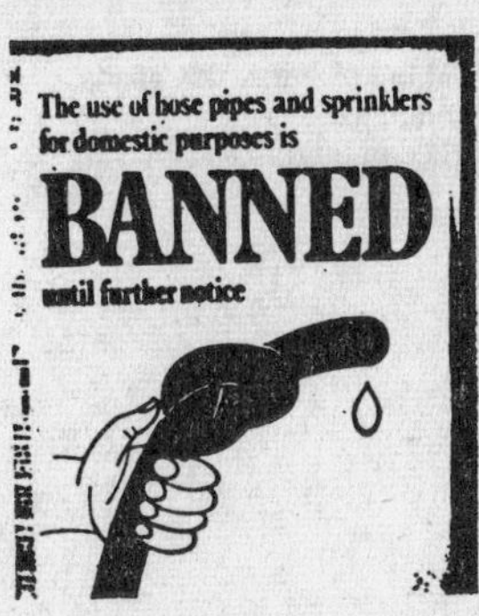

banned: forbidden

MALICIOUS° DAMAGE

Most passengers respect London Transport property, which is for their use and convenience, but there is a small minority who does not. It is an offence wilfully or maliciously to damage London Transport property, and this includes bus stops and shelters, and the posters and timetables which they carry.

OFFENDERS WILL BE PROSECUTED AND THE PENALTIES ARE SEVERE

(London Transport)

malicious: intentional – in the bad sense

First prize for the dumbest° comment on the Quebec° election goes to Bill Vander Zalm, minister of human resources in the government of British Columbia. Three cheers if Quebec separates from Canada, he said – then your corn flakes° will be cheaper because they won't have to be labelled bilingually°.

(*Vancouver Sun*)

dumbest: most stupid
Quebec: the French-speaking province of Canada
corn flakes: breakfast food in packets
labelled bilingually: marked in English *and* French

What did you drink in the Great War, Daddy?

Once in enemy hands, what privations° a prisoner of war had to suffer. But even in the direst° situation, British ingenuity° and sense of humour could overcome the cruellest indignities° – such as being deprived° of one's Port.

The following message was received by postcard on 1 September 1915 from a Captain, held prisoner of war at Friedburg Hessen in Germany.

> *Will you go to my chemist in Denmark Street and tell him to send me some of his Red Eye Lotion, the prescription° of Dr Sandeman in 1905. Have this put in a blue poison bottle and labelled pharmaceutically° and put it in plenty of cardboard in a wooden box.*

Today such an officer would send for Sandeman Partners' Port. It is the finest old port, matured in wood, and ready for drinking this year.

Advertisement for Sandeman Partners' Port)

privations: losses
direst: most serious
ingenuity: cleverness
indignities: humiliations
deprived: made to do without
prescription: directions for making (usually a medicine)
pharmaceutically: as if from a chemist's

If Niagara Falls couldn't leak° into our packaging what chance does a little rain have?

What you see actually happened.

It took place on a bitterly cold day in November 1975.

Visibility° was poor. The temperature was −3°C. And below us 34 million gallons of water a minute thundered down the 51-m falls.

Conditions seemed perfect for testing the weather-resistant qualities of packaging made from Tri-Wall Pak material.

So that's what we did. We loaded fragile° Royal Brierly cut-glass into a Tri-Wall Pak box and surrounded it with dry rock salt.

Then we heaved° the pack into the torrent°, watched it as it sailed towards the brink° and held our breath as it shot over.

A mile downstream it was pulled out and taken ashore. All the glassware in the box was unbroken and there was dry salt inside.

All of which we think testifies° to the fact that you can't get tougher, more weather-resistant packaging than Tri-Wall Pak.

(Tri-Wall Pak, London)

leak: get through
visibility: the distance one can see
fragile: easily broken
heaved: threw
torrent: fast flowing river
brink: edge
testifies (to the fact that): proves

As part of a stunt° to demonstrate the toughness of Permatuff glass, Mr Robinson, who holds the Guinness Book of Records title for the heaviest man in Great Britain (he weighs 233 kg), invited a young lady to dance on a glass table with him. Even with both of them on top of it, the glass didn't crack.

(*South Kensington & Chelsea News*)

stunt: trick, exhibition

[This extract is taken from a popular radio programme, My Word, in which the speakers have to invent explanations for the origin of popular sayings and quotations.]

'Where there's a will, there's a way'
(G. Herbert, 1640)

When it finally became apparent that the entertainment business was the only career for which I was suited, I went to a large cinema in Leicester Square and begged them to take me on in any capacity°.

'You want to start at the very bottom of the ladder°?' asked the manager. I nodded. He pointed to something leaning against the wall. 'There's the ladder.'

The new job was rather grandly titled 'Head of Display'. All it really involved was climbing up the ladder and fixing, high on the front wall of the cinema, those large metal letters which spell out the name of the film on that week.

I can't say it was a glamorous° task. In a high wind, it was often difficult and – artistically – it was something less than fulfilling. Unlike a painter or sculptor, I was in no position to step back and survey my finished work. This led, in the first few weeks, to certain errors° of judgement, among which I can remember WEST SIDE SORTY, THE SNOUD OF MUSIC and SANE CONNERY IN GLODFINGER.

Nevertheless, the work did make me feel that little bit nearer to the great throbbing heart of show business.

But it is only the moment of emergency° which really proves our worth. My moment came when the telephone rang at three o'clock one morning. It was the manager. 'I have just passed the cinema on my way home,' he said. 'Your Y has dropped off.'

Fuddled° with sleep as I was, I immediately understood why he was so concerned. The film we were showing that week was *My Fair Lady*. Although the movement towards free thinking was gathering strength, it was still not acceptable for a Leicester Square cinema to appear to be showing a film called *My Fair Lad*°.

When I reached the cinema, I found the letter Y lying broken on the pavement. Obviously, it was ruined beyond repair. I hurried to the store-room where the spare letters were kept. There was no spare Y!

Perhaps I can construct one, I thought. Perhaps I could take an X and change it into a Y by sawing off the – as it were – south-east leg? No luck. I did it all right, but it wouldn't stay up on the wall. Where, in London, at four o'clock in the morning, can one lay hands on a 1.25 metre-tall letter Y?

To my good luck, the cinema on the opposite side of Leicester Square was showing a film whose title contained the letter I wanted. As at that time of the morning people get up to all sorts of strange things in the West End, nobody even paused to stare when I climbed up and removed the enormous Y. The only nasty moment came when I was carrying it across Coventry Street. A policeman stopped me. 'Excuse me, sir. What might you be doing walking along at 4.30 a.m. carrying a four-foot letter Y?'

Fortunately, I kept my presence of mind. 'This is not a letter Y, officer,' I said. 'It's a water-divining rod°.' He even touched his helmet to me as he went on his way.

By 5.00 a.m. the fair name of *My Fair Lady* had been restored. True, the cinema opposite, which had been packing them in with a magnificent film starring Gregory Peck and Orson Welles, now appeared to be showing a film called MOB DICK°. But that's show business.

I've had warm feelings towards the screen version of Herman

Melville's great novel ever since. Indeed, I recommend that any other Head of Display who finds himself in a similar predicament to mine should look around for a cinema showing it. You'll find what I found: *Where there's a whale, there's a Y.*

(Denis Norden, *The My Word stories*)

capacity: position, job
at the bottom of the ladder: (idiomatic) in the lowest job
glamorous: interesting exciting
errors: mistakes
emergency: needing immediate attention
fuddled: confused
lad: boy
water-divining rod: a branch shaped like a Y, used for discovering underground water
Mob Dick: Moby Dick, Melville's novel about a great white whale

6 Cashing in

The bitterness of poor quality will be remembered long after the joy of a low price.

(Sign in a shop)

Money is the root of all evil

(Proverb)

'It is a peculiarity° of the sentiment of patriotism° that men can be more easily persuaded to sacrifice their lives for their country than to sacrifice the contents of their pockets.'

(Robert Thouless, *Straight and crooked thinking*)

peculiarity: special quality
patriotism: love of one's country

Change a Pound for £1.34

A one-pound National Savings Certificate grows to £1.34 in four years.

We guarantee it, four years in advance. With no ifs, ands, or buts about it. Your interest° of 34p in the pound won't go up or down.

That's equivalent to 7.59 % over the full term° of four years.

Free of all UK income tax and capital gains tax, with nothing to declare on your tax return°.

Buy certificates at your Bank or Post Office. And get a guarantee of interest for a change.

(Department for National Savings, London)

interest: money paid for sums of money left in savings accounts
term: period
tax return: form on which you declare how much you earn

POUND TAKES A TUMBLE
(*The Sun*, 16.12.76)

POUND CONTINUES TO FALL
(*Toronto Globe & Mail*, 28.10.76)

POUND GAINS BY A CENT
(*The Guardian*, 21.12.76)

Reserves reach lowest since '71
(*Australasian Express*, London, 26.11.76)

Loan Rumour Boosts Pound
(*Yorkshire Post*, 30.10.76)

Australian Dollar moves up Unaided
(*The Australian*, 30.12.76)

Sinking pound slips down again
(*Yorkshire Post*, 7.10.76)

A terrible story reaches me from Hong Kong. It appears that a British businessman, staying at one of the more luxurious° hotels, requested a girl to be brought up to his room.

Having made the delivery, the bellboy° heard a piercing scream. Returning to the room, he found the girl in a corner, her arm outstretched in terror. 'Help me, help me!' she cried. 'He wants to pay me in sterling!°'

(*The Sunday Times*)

luxurious: expensive
bellboy: porter
sterling: English pounds

Deadly guards circle Ceylon jewels

Three poisonous snakes, whose bite could kill a person in 10 minutes, are guarding a blue star sapphire° worth nearly £300,000 at an exhibition of gems° from Sri Lanka.

'Normally it would be forbidden to let these poisonous snakes guard exhibition objects, but it's different in this case because the gems are being displayed at an Embassy,' a police official said.

Exhibition officials said that a person bitten by one of these snakes would require at least 80 ml of an anti-poison serum° to survive. Serum was being kept ready at a nearby hospital.

Hundreds of star sapphires

and other dazzling gems worth a total of one million pounds are on display behind glass. Visitors attracted by the blue star sapphire gasped when they spotted the 60-cm-long brown guards. According to legend, ancient kings of Ceylon had their tresaure guarded by snakes.

(*Yorkshire Post*)

sapphire: precious stone used in making jewellery
gems: precious stones
serum: liquid for injections

RENT ALLOWANCE SCHEME FOR PRIVATE TENANTS OF FURNISHED AND UNFURNISHED DWELLINGS in *the Royal Borough of Kensington and Chelsea*

The government have made the following changes in the above scheme, effective in relation to any week beginning after 14 November 1976.

How do these changes affect you?

(*a*) If you have never claimed before, or if you have claimed and been told you do not qualify, you may now be eligible° for a rent allowance. You are strongly recommended to seek advice or ask for an application form at the address shown below, particularly if you are unemployed, ill, or on a low income, or if you have a large family.
(*b*) If you are already in receipt of° a rent allowance, no action is required by you, unless there have been any changes in your circumstances since you were last assessed.

The Council are particularly anxious that no person should forego° their right to a rent allowance because they do not understand the Scheme or because they have difficulty in completing the application form. They are also concerned that no person should be deterred° from making an application for fear that their personal details may improperly become known. All possible assistance will be given by the Housing Department and each application is treated as STRICTLY PRIVATE AND CONFIDENTIAL.

Example of rent allowance calculation

Family: Husband and wife with two dependent children
Income: Husband's earnings £80 per week

Family allowance:	£1.50 per week		
Maximum rent:	£18.00		
Minimum rent:	20 % of £18.00 = £3.60		
	Income £81.50		
Needs allowance, husband and wife plus two children			
	£43.45		
	£38.05 × 17 % of excess =	plus	£6.47
		rent	10.07
		allowance	7.93
		maximum rent	£18.00

(*South Kensington & Chelsea News*)

eligible: having the right to apply
in receipt of: getting
forego: give up
deterred: put off

Europe's bargain basement°

The prospect is that Britain is likely to be Europe's bargain basement for some time to come. London has long enjoyed a reputation for quality, of course, but until recently it benefited only the select few to whom Harrods, Fortnum and Mason, Jaeger, and Savile Row were revered° names. The move from class° to mass started with the beginning of cheap air travel, the rise of European incomes, and the fame of such trendy° designers as Mary Quant and the people in Carnaby Street.

But it was not until the pound sank last year that the great shopping spree° really started.

Just how much can a European save by shopping in England? The answers vary from country to country. Clearly, however, savings are likely to be largest for Europeans living closest to the Channel ports: they can make a day trip by sea for a few pounds, and by spending as little as £50, more than recover their expenses.

'Foreign shopping is certainly a long-run trend°,' said one of the directors of Jaeger, 'but the pace° at which it will develop depends greatly on how people are treated in hotels, restaurants and other public places.'

Language is one of the problems. In the West End of London, certainly, the bigger stores have interpreters. But at too many shops, hotels and restaurants the only language is English, unless the foreigner is fortunate enough to meet a compatriot° working there. An amusing example of a typical problem is told by Susie Orde, Savoy Hotel's public relations director. A Japanese businessman with his interpreter, came in search of the Savoy's own blend° of coffee.

Interpreter: 'He wants ten tons.'

Assistant; 'Ah yes: ten tins at £1.60 each is £16.'

Interpreter: 'No, no, please – ten tons.'

Miss Orde has to work this out on her electronic calculator (Japanese): 'But that's £35,840,' she gasps.

Interpreter: 'Yes, he have many friends.'

(*The Sunday Telegraph Magazine*)

bargain basement: part of the shop where very cheap goods are sold
revered: respected
class: quality
trendy: fashionable
spree: spending a lot of money
trend: movement
pace: speed
compatriot: fellow countryman
blend: mixture

Let off steam°

It makes me mad to read how much money people have been spending on Booze° this week. I'm seventy-three, and by the time I've paid my rent I have about £3 of my pension left to live on.

This is less than most people are apparently spending every week on alcohol.

Mrs Evelyn Jones, Winchester

Why should people work harder when there is absolutely no incentive° to do so? My son worked all weekend recently to help out his boss – only to have about two thirds of his overtime° taken away in tax.

Mrs E. Jones, Lancs.

Hasn't the time come to call a halt to the annual° farce° of giving Christmas boxes°?

In the days when public servants were underpaid, this was an appropriate° way to show one's appreciation.

But now that dustmen and the like° are paid the proper rate for the job, they're often better off than the people who are expected to tip° them. Come to think of it, they ought to tip *us*!

Mr William Thomas, Manchester

(*Sunday Mirror*)

let off steam: say what you think, get rid of your anger
booze: (slang) liquor
incentive: urge, good reason
overtime: extra work (usually higher paid)
annual: yearly
farce: stupid custom
Christmas box: money (tip) given to people such as dustmen, postmen, milkmen, etc. before the Christmas holidays
appropriate: suitable
the like: people who perform public services
tip: give money for 'service'

Australian of the Year

MY nomination° is the over-burdened° Australian tax-payer. As the victim of perhaps the most oppressive° middle-income tax scale in the world, he cannot even afford to drown his sorrows° in our overtaxed drink.

In spite of all this, he still preserves a childlike belief that although he has been deceived° by successive° governments, some day some government will actually reduce taxation. This faith is deserving of recognition.

Alan H. Robson
NSW

(*The Australian*)

nomination: (literally = naming) choice
over-burdened: with too many duties and responsibilities
oppressive: unbearable, crushing
drown (his) sorrows: (idiomatic) drown (your) sorrows = forget (your) problems
deceived: misled
successive: one after the other

DO YOU ONLY GIVE PRESENTS TO PEOPLE WHO GIVE PRESENTS TO YOU?

All things being equal, you may very well ask 'Why not'?

But things, of course, are very far from equal.

While we pore over° diet sheets°, millions are starving to death.

While we complain about the NHS°, some countries have only one doctor for every 15,000 people.

While we argue about comprehensive schools, the majority in undeveloped countries can't read or write.

Christian Aid is doing all a charity° can do.

Which is to put the money you give us to the best possible use. (We would always rather teach a family to farm than hand out bowls of soup.)

Like Britain, the poor world is suffering badly from inflation°. All the same, money still goes further there.

The price of a toy train set can still finance transport for a doctor.

The price of a child's nurse's outfit° can still train a medical assistant.

It needn't take a lot to give something to those who have so little this Christmas.

(Advertisement for Christian Aid, London)

pore over: study carefully
diet sheets: ways of losing weight
NHS: National Health Service
charity: organization for giving money, clothes and help to the poor
inflation: rise in prices together with a drop in the value of money
outfit: uniform, instruments, etc. for the child to play being a nurse

It's not what you've got, it's the way you spend it

I myself have mixed feelings about money. It doesn't, of course, buy friends, though it does allow you a better class of enemy, and there are few sorrows in which a good income can be of no avail°. Any fool can make money, but spending it in style° is more difficult.

Diamond Jim Brady used to light his cigar with a dollar bill, and this is very bad style indeed. It's vulgar and pointless, and the smell of burning dollar bills would probably ruin even an American cigar.

Revengeful° spending, however, can have style. Lord Nuffield once wanted to join a certain golf club, but some of the members objected. So he bought the whole club, and only elected° the members who had smiled upon him. I think that's nice.

I recall with affection the standards set by my friend Charlie Cringleford. He was by no account° a rich man, but he was a very pretty spender all the same. When he was in the Army he used to send his shirts home every week from India to be washed. And his soldier servant once found a note on the dresser° saying, 'Please put two bottles of the Cockburn '12° by my bedside and call me the day after tomorrow.'

I also greatly admire Sir Joseph Camps, who may possibly not be known to you. He it was who refused to accompany Captain Cook on his trip to Australia unless he was allowed to take with him not one but two horn players to entertain him during dinner. There's richness for you!

(From an article by Lord Mancroft in *The Punch guide to good living*)

(of no) avail: (no) use, help
in style: with good taste and without worrying about the amount spent
revengeful: to harm others who have hurt you
elected: allowed to be members of the club again
by no account: not at all
dresser: small cupboard
Cockburn '12: expensive wine

Split personality

A FRENCHMAN who spent 11 years in a Toulouse mental hospital, being treated as a schizophrenic°, claims that he was held by mistake in place of someone with the same name. He is suing° the hospital for one million francs (£120,000)

(*Yorkshire Post*)

schizophrenic: person suffering from mental disturbance
suing: demanding money from them in court

*

Song of sixpence

IN HIS WILL°, Abraham Litvinski left his entire £600,000 to the Tel Aviv Zoo and the Israeli Society for the Prevention of Cruelty to Animals. His brother, Haim, a lawyer, is contesting° the will. Abraham left Haim the sum of sixpence.

(*Yorkshire Post*)

will: legal document stating what should happen to one's property after one's death
contesting: fighting against it in court

*

Well-heeled°

A woman rushed to a cobbler's° shop in Nice yesterday to recover the £2,000 savings she had left in a boot that was to be repaired.

(*Daily Mirror*)

well-heeled: (play on words): (1) rich; (2) shoes with strong heels
cobbler's: shoemaker's

Money left to Jesus in will°

LONDON – Mr Ernest Digweed has caused a posthumous° sensation by leaving all his money to Jesus.

The retired schoolteacher's will turns over £20,000 to a Government Agency to invest° for 80 years.

'If during those 80 years the Lord Jesus Christ shall come to reign on Earth, then the Public Trustee°, upon obtaining proof which shall satisfy them of His identity, shall pay to the Lord Jesus Christ all the property which they hold on his behalf°', says the will.

After 80 years the money must go to the Crown.

Mr Digweed died in Portsmouth aged 81.

No one has yet come forward to claim the money, said Mr Joseph Radford, the assistant public trustee. If someone did, 'it is something on which we shall have to be advised by our solicitors°.'

(*Associated Press*)

will: document stating who is to receive a person's money/property after his/her death
posthumous: after death
invest: put money into something in order to gain more money at a later date
Public Trustee: Government agency controlling the money
on his behalf: (legal expression) for him
solicitors: lawyers

When Eugene Schneider's wife sued° him for divorce and claimed her right to half his property in New Jersey, he decided to give her exactly that.

He used an electric saw to cut their 80,000-dollar wooden home down the middle, and then divided the family car the same way.

(*The Sunday Times*, Johannesburg)

sued: took him to court

The lazy man's way to riches

'Most people are too busy earning a living to make any money.'

I used to work hard. The 18-hour days. The seven-day weeks.

But I didn't start making big money until I did less – a lot less.

For example, this ad° took about two hours to write. It has already earned me over $100,000 in America and, with a little luck, should earn me even more here. What's more, I'm going to ask you to send me £4 for something that cost me no more than 20p. After all, why should you care if I make a £3.80 profit if I can show you how to make a lot more?

I'm going to tell you what it took me 11 years to perfect: How to Make Money the Lazy Man's Way. O.K. – now I have to brag° a little. I don't mind it. And it's necessary to prove that sending me £4, which I'll keep uncashed° until you're satisfied, is the smartest thing you ever did.

I live in a home that's worth £40,000. My 'office' about a mile and a half from my home is right on the beach. I do about six hours work a day, eight or nine months a year. The rest of the time we spend at our mountain 'cabin'. I paid £12,000 for it – cash. I have two boats and a Cadillac. All paid for.

And I'll show you how I did it – the Lazy Man's Way – a secret I've shared with just a few friends till now.

It doesn't require 'education'. I only went to high school.

It doesn't require 'capital'°.

It doesn't require 'luck'. I've had more than my share, but I'm not promising that you'll make as much money as I have. And you may do better.

It doesn't require 'talent'. Just enough brains to know what to look for.

It doesn't require 'youth'.

It doesn't require 'experience'.

What does it require? Belief. Enough to take a chance. Enough to put the principles into *action.* If you do just that – nothing more, nothing less – the results *will* be hard to believe. Remember – I promise it.

The wisest man I ever knew told me something I never forgot: 'Most people are too busy earning a living to make any money.'

Don't take as long as I did to find out that he was right.

I'll prove it to you, if you'll send in the coupon now. Just try it. If I'm wrong, all you've lost is a couple of minutes and an 8½p stamp. But what if I'm right?

Joe Karbo, 1 Whitehall Place, London SW1

Joe, you may be full of hot air°, but what have I got to lose? Send me the Lazy Man's Way to Riches. *But don't deposit my cheque or postal order for 31 days after it's in the mail.*

If I return your material – for *any* reason – within that time, return my *uncashed* cheque or postal order to me. On that basis, here's my £4.

Name ....

Address ....

ad: advertisement
brag: boast
uncashed: not changed into money
capital: money
hot air: nonsense

Get-rich-quick plan branded as phoney°

A province-wide, direct mail get-rich-quick scheme has been branded as 'phoney° as a $3 bill°' by the Vancouver Better Business Bureau.

Thousands of homes throughout British Columbia have been mailed a pamphlet° offering 'the opportunity of a lifetime'. Recipients° are urged to send $3.15 to a Vancouver Post Office box number for the chance to earn up to $1,600 a month in their spare time or $8,000 a month working overseas.

The mailed-out pamphlets are headed International Financial Association of Family Improvement, Bental Centre, Telephone 985–1683, Vancouver. Repeated phone calls to the number were unanswered.

'This is your big chance to solve your financial problems,' the three-page pamphlet says. People joining the association also get the chance to take part in a lottery° offering prizes up to $150,000. 'We believe this is the only existing lottery where you don't have to buy tickets to win,' the pamphlet continues.

Mr Forbes, chief of the Better Business Bureau, said, 'It's obvious that the only people who are going to make anything out of this are those who are organizing it. He also warned of a second get-rich-quick scheme operating in Bental Centre. Letters have been sent to people with surnames Hansen and Miller, telling them they may be going to inherit° a fortune.

Recipients are told that, if they are related to a 'Tom Hansen' of Stockton, California, 'there may be some possibility that you could be entitled to an inheritance'. People are asked to send $10 to United Heir° Search, PO Box 8482, Stockton.

(*Vancouver Sun*)

branded as phoney: described as dishonest
$3 bill: there is no paper note worth $3
pamphlet: advertising brochure
recipients: those who get (the pamphlet)
lottery: game of chance (usually run by the state); tickets with numbers are sold – some of the numbers win cash prizes
inherit: receive money or property from someone after his death
heir: person with a right to property

Notice to Creditors°

In the estate° of William Bell, deceased°.

All persons having claim against the Estate of William Bell, late° of the City of Mississauga, in the Regional Municipality of Peel, who died on 15 March 1975, are hereby notified to send particulars of same to the undersigned on or before 11 November 1976, after which date the Estate will be distributed, and the undersigned will not be liable° to any person of whose claim they shall not then have notice.

DATED at Toronto this eighth day of October 1976

(*Toronto Globe & Mail*)

creditors: people to whom money is owed by someone else
estate: property (of a dead person)
deceased: (legal term) dead
late: (legal term) recently, i.e. when he was alive
liable: responsible

The Bee

The bee is a merchant.
He trades among
flower plants.

(Peter Kelso)

The world's richest country

To reach the world's richest country, you don't set out for the Middle East, but for the South Pacific, to a tiny speck° just south of the Equator, called Nauru. Only 8.2 square miles in size, the whole of this island state can be seen from the air as the plane comes in to land. It looks like an upturned soup dish, the raised part brown and pitted° and the rim° deep green, ringed by a coral beach. The blue South Pacific stretches for thousands of miles in all directions, the nearest piece of land being Ocean Island 200 miles to the east. But that too is only a speck in the middle of nowhere.

Nauru is so small that the plane lands in what is best described as the capital's main street. The seaward side of the runway° has traffic lights at each end to stop cars when planes are landing. The tiny air terminal is crowded with well-fed and brightly clothed Naurans with their smart cars. New arrivals are driven off in Japanese minibuses for the 10-minute drive half way round the island to the only hotel, the luxurious Menen. The well-paved road passes rows of neat, modern houses, set among the trees.

An idyllic° picture. And with Naurans now earning an average of $22,500 a year (compared with $12,000 for Kuwait), the island's 6,000 inhabitants would seem to have little to worry about. A trip to the island's central hump° tells a slightly different story.

The hump is Nauru's wealth – a near solid mound of phosphate° round which the island's entire economy revolves°, and without which Nauru would be one of the world's most wretched° islands instead of its richest.

When Nauru became independent from Britain in 1968, it took over the mining of the phosphate. About 40 million tons of the original 100 million tons of phosphate were left. Since then it has extracted° another 10 million tons, which leaves enough for another 20–25 years.

The force behind Nauru is its 54-year-old President Hammer de Roburt. He clearly enjoys his role as leader of one of the world's quaintest° states, but avoids the foreign Press, perhaps because Nauru is a country that can easily be made fun of. He has kept Nauru out of both the UN and the

Commonwealth, and, in fact, the island's only evident link with another country is through its currency, the Australian dollar.

One of his worries is what to do about the centre of the island which, after nearly 80 years of mining, looks like a giant's bone yard with its yellowing coral rock picked clean by the excavators°. His most important task, though, is to secure the country's future once the phosphate runs out. Some of the country's money is being used to buy up property, mainly in Australia, where Nauru now owns a large part of downtown Melbourne. Not surprisingly, therefore, it has been seriously suggested that once the phosphate runs out, Naurans should all pack their bags and leave for their estates in Australia.

(David Lascelles, *The Financial Times*)

speck: spot
pitted: full of small holes
rim: edge
runway: landing strip (for aeroplanes)
idyllic: perfect
hump: hill
phosphate: mineral
revolves: centres, depends
wretched: unfortunate
extracted: taken out
quaintest: oddest, strangest
excavators: machines for digging

How much do you give?

Do you spend 47p on a packet of cigarettes on your way to church and put the 3p change in the collection° ?

Or do you put 10p in the collection and then spend £1 on a round of drinks afterwards?

Do you spend £300 on a foreign holiday and put £1 in the collection?

Do you spend £1 coming to church by taxi and put 5p in the collection?

Perhaps you have an evening out with a friend for £20 and put 20p in the collection?

Or maybe you spend £200 on school fees and rattle a bunch of keys over the collection bag, pretending that you are getting rid of all your change.

If you do, now is the time to turn over a

new leaf° and help St Augustine's Church to get back on its financial feet. And if the £900 target is reached, it will prevent the Church going into the red°.

(*South Kensington & Chelsea News*)

collection: money taken during the church service
turn over a new leaf: change your habits, improve
going into the red: getting into debt

If you had to economise°, what is the first thing you'd give up – and the last?

I would give up cigarettes so that I could continue to go to bingo°.

I would give up anything – I would cheerfully miss a couple of meals – rather than give up my investments in the pools°.

My weekly 50p buys me one of the most precious things – hope. I daydream not of living in luxury°, but of giving my husband and boys what they need – a house with a garden, instead of being cramped in a flat.

Mrs M. S. Manchester

We have decided we would first of all do without chocolates and sweets. It would take a lot of doing, but we would try.

The last thing we would cut would be what we spend on clothes and make-up. If we didn't look smart and pretty we would stand no chance with the boys.

Anne and Lynda, Overton-on-Dee, Clwyd

As I'm a bit on the big side, I would cut down on food. The last thing I'd give up would be tomato sauce. I love it on everything.

Miss F. King, Battersea, London

I would stop buying biscuits before I gave up buying flowers.

Mrs P. West, Dawlish, Devon

I would gladly not go away for a summer holiday. I always come back depressed by the prospect° of returning to my daily routine. The last thing I'd give up would be my fortnightly visit to the wrestling° matches. I shout and scream and come away tension-free.

Mrs M. Francis, Bristol

I could do without bingo, but not without perfume. I don't feel dressed without it.

Mrs Gerda Greenwood, Kent

I would start by cancelling my rented colour TV agreement. The last thing I would part with would be my radio. I would find life without music unbearable.

H. Bennett, Kent

Now the cold nights are coming, I could easily stop going to bingo. I would not as easily do without my fish-and-chips lunch on Saturday.

Mrs P. Hall, Sydenham, London

Giving up meat would cut down my food bills dramatically. The last things I would give up would be good bras°. I would be in misery without them.

Miss G. Fenn, Halifax

I'd give up my weekly 50p flutter° on the horses. I never win, anyway. But I couldn't do without my electric blanket.

Mrs P. Greensmith, Nottingham

The first thing to go would be my television set. The very last thing I'd part with would be my dog. He senses my every mood. When I'm feeling ill he puts his head on my lap°. If I cry, he puts his face against mine to comfort me.

Mrs D. Williamson, Hillingdon

(*The Sun*)

economise: save
bingo: a popular game
pools: a way of winning money by guessing the result of football matches
luxury: great comfort
prospect: idea, thought
wrestling: sport in which two people fight using the whole body
bras: woman's underclothing
flutter: money risked on horse-racing
lap: legs, above the knees

A day in the life of a tourist trap

Stratford-upon-Avon is England's biggest tourist trap outside London. A happy accident of birth more than 400 years ago now attracts a million and a half visitors each year – and 10 million pounds of their money – to what would be otherwise an unremarkable town (population 19,000). This year, on Shakespeare's birthday, *The Sunday Times Magazine* spent a day in Stratford. Here we describe some of the things that happened on that day.

4 a.m. Mrs Lyn Hobbs, 29, decides she'd better not leave it any longer. She's been through this before. She wakes her husband. Henry Hobbs gets the car out and they drive to the Maternity Home°. Shakespeare isn't the only one who's going to have a birthday today.

> Eddie Golding, former carpenter, lives in retirement in a cottage facing the theatre. He says: 'I don't go to the theatre now. I can't stand Shakespeare. After all, I had 42 years with the bugger.'

5.48 Sunrise. The weather forecast promises sunny intervals, isolated showers, wind NE moderate or fresh; maximum temperature 12°C.

6.00 The morning shift° comes on duty at the town's ambulance station. There's an average of five emergency° calls a day.

6.50 Christopher McHendry sets off for his job as a butcher in Stratford. Near the village of Clifford Chambers his van smashes into a tree. A passing lorry driver runs for a telephone.

7.15 The queue is growing outside the Royal Shakespeare Theatre for tickets to the evening performance of *Much Ado About Nothing*. Each morning at 10.30, a few standing room places are sold along with the returned tickets.

8.00 The American flag was hoisted° the wrong way up today at the Hilton Hotel, but Paula Catterson starts her work as chambermaid as usual. She has been there for two years and has had her share of embarrassing° moments: 'You knock on the door, a voice says come in, and the next thing you know there's a man coming towards you without a stitch on°. You get out quick . . .' It takes about 25 minutes to clean the room. 'The Japanese are the best' says Paula. 'They are the cleanest and tidiest guests. The Americans are by far the untidiest.'

8.10 Friday is market day in Stratford, and the first shoppers are already out. A sign on Mick Robbins' stall says: 'We sell the best, the others sell the rest.' It may not be the best verse to come out of Stratford, but an elderly man is sufficiently impressed to spend 95p.

9.00 Joseph Nelson opens up the Gents section of the Waterside Lavatories. Joseph says he sometimes has queues forming to get in and that he ends up 'rushing about with toilet rolls all day'.

10.20 Sister Valerie Young delivers Mrs Hobbs' baby. It's a girl.

10.30 Fire call. The fire engines hurry down to the riverside. It's a false alarm°.

12.30 The offices of the *Stratford Herald* are deserted except for the editor, Les Emes. He is on his own because half of his staff have gone to visit a school at Shipton. Half of his staff means two people. 'The tourists rarely make° our pages,' says Les. 'Unless a tourist falls into the river and drowns, we don't write about them.'

13.25 Neils Sonner, a librarian from New York City, is standing outside Shakespeare's birthplace in Henley Street. He has lost his wife and the rest of his party. He slowly realises he has also lost his coach back to London. 'It happens every day,' says a local tour organiser.

(*The Sunday Times Magazine*)

Maternity Home: hospital where children are born
shift: team of workers
emergency: needing immediate attention
hoisted: raised
embarrassing: awkward, difficult
without a stitch on: naked
false alarm: the caller was playing a joke
make: appear on

7 Take it easy

Section Q. – The mind

The Greek word 'psyche' means the 'soul' or 'mind' and the science concerned with the study of the mind and mental processes is called *psychology*.

The branch of medicine concerned with disorders° of mental processes is termed *psychiatry*, or psychological medicine.

Among the most important types of mental disorder encountered° in psychiatric practice are:

(*a*) *Subnormality* – a condition in which development of the mind is incomplete and intelligence is below normal. Subnormality may result from hereditary° factors, or disease or injury affecting the developing brain during foetal life° or childhood.

(*b*) *Psychoneuroses* (neuroses) – these are disorders of mental function which affect large numbers of the population. While° they do not produce any complete breakdown of mental processes, and affected° patients often possess considerable insight° into their own psychological problems, they may produce serious effects, both mental and physical, and adverse° effects on work efficiency.

Some examples of disorders classified as psychoneuroses are: *anxiety° states, obsessive-compulsive neuroses, hysteria and behaviour disorders of childhood.*

(*c*) *Psychoses* – severe disorders of mental function in which the patient's insight into his own psychological problems may be impaired° or lost. They produce a marked° breakdown of mental processes, which in some of these conditions is of a temporary nature but in others is permanent.

(P. Davies, *Medical terminology in hospital practice*)

disorders: disturbances
encountered: found, met with

hereditary: passed on from parents or grandparents
foetal (life): before birth, while the child is still being formed
while: although
affected: suffering from neurosis
insights (into): understanding (of)
adverse: bad
anxiety: worry
impaired: damaged
marked: noticeable

CENTRAL INTAKE HOSPITAL

Admittance sheet Friday, 15 August 1969

Name ....Unknown
Sex ....Male
Age ....Unknown
Address..........Unknown

General remarks

. . . At midnight the police found Patient wandering on the Embankment near Waterloo Bridge. They took him into the station thinking he was drunk or drugged. Brought him to us at 3 a.m. by ambulance. During admittance° Patient attempted several times to lie down on the desk. He seemed to think it was a boat or a raft°. Police are checking ports, ships, etc. Patient was well dressed but had not changed his clothes for some time. He did not seem very hungry or thirsty. He had no papers or money or marks of identity. Police think he was robbed. He is an educated man. He was given two Libriums° but did not sleep. He was talking loudly. Patient was moved into the small Observation ward as he was disturbing the other patients.

NIGHT NURSE 6 a.m.

Nothing from police. No reports of any small boats, yachts, or swimmers unaccounted for°. Patient continues talking aloud, singing, swinging back and forth in bed. He is excessively fatigued°.

DOCTOR *X* 17 August

Patient very disturbed. Asked his name: Jason. He is on a raft in the Atlantic. Will see him tomorrow.

DOCTOR *Y*

Doctor *Y*: Did you sleep well?
Patient: I kept dropping off°, but I mustn't, I must not.
Doctor *Y*: But why not? I want you to.
Patient: I'd slide off into the deep sea swells.
Doctor *Y*: No you won't. That's a very comfortable bed, and you're in a nice quiet room.
Patient: Bed of the sea. Deep sea bed.
Doctor *Y*: You aren't on a raft. You aren't on the sea. You aren't a sailor.
Patient: I'm not a sailor?
Doctor *Y*: You are in the Central Intake Hospital, in bed, being looked after. You must rest. We want you to sleep.
Patient: If I sleep I'll die.
Doctor *Y*: What's your name? Will you tell me?
Patient: Jonah.
Doctor *Y*: Yesterday it was Jason. You can't be either, you know.
Patient: We are all sailors.
Doctor *Y*: I am not. I'm a doctor in this hospital.
Patient: If I'm not a sailor then you aren't a doctor.
Doctor *Y*: Very well. But you are making yourself very tired. Lie down. Take a rest. Try not to talk so much.
Patient: I'm not talking to you, am I? Around and around and around and around and around and around and around and around and around and around and around . . .
Nurse: You've been going around and around and around for hours now, did you know that . . . Around and around what? Where? There now, turn over.
Patient: It's very hot. I'm not far away from the equator.
Nurse: You're still on the raft, then?
Patient: *You* aren't.
Nurse: I can't say that I am.
Patient: Then how can you be talking to me?

Nurse: Do try and lie easy. We don't want you to get so terribly tired.

(Doris Lessing, *Briefing for a descent into hell*)

during admittance: while his form was being filled in
raft: flat 'boat', usually made of logs (e.g. Kon-Tiki)
Libriums: tranquillizers
unaccounted for: missing
fatigued: very tired
dropping off: falling asleep

WORRIED?
Never mind, it's probably nothing to be worried about

There are national differences in anxiety°. Comparison of the frequency of suicide°, alcoholism, mental illness, heart disease and calorie intake° (the more anxious you are the less you eat) shows that the Japanese and the Germans worry the most. Britain comes a modest seventeenth in the Anxious Nations Cup, which offers little comfort to those who view anxiety as a simple reflection of economic depression°.

(from J. Nicholson in *New Society*, quoted in the *Vancouver Sun*)

anxiety: worry and fear
suicide: killing oneself
calorie intake: the amount you eat
(economic) depression: bad times (financially)

Let's slow down

This *Monthly Letter* does not set itself up as a confident counsellor° in mental and physical health, but merely attempts to break down a problem facing every adult person in Canada. The problem is the feeling of being pushed. We are full of tension°. We have difficulty in relaxing°. We feel that we are not quite as quick as we should be in understanding things. We are sensitive and doubtful and in a hurry. We have no time for rest.

Worry is commonly blamed for this. Strangely enough, it is often not the things we do but the things we don't get done that worry us. We worry about the past, which can't be helped, and about the future, without being able to change it. Many times worry is the cause and not the result of problems.

We all know the story of the centipede° that became worried about a possible breakdown of the mechanism moving his 100 legs, and ended in a mess. A trainman tells the story of a woman who burst into tears when the train was crossing a bridge over a flooded river. He questioned her sympathetically about her trouble, and she told him: 'I was just thinking how terrible it would be if I had a child and it was drowned.'

Silly? But how much more sensible are the things *we* worry about?

The man who keeps his balance realises that he cannot do and have everything he would like. Time, ability and opportunity limit what is possible. To many people, time taken for rest seems a total loss. Adults, like children, can find many excuses for not going to bed; yet we all need rest.

It is not only time in bed, however, that counts as resting. Short periods of relaxation throughout the day result in far less fatigue° than when one attempts to carry on for a long time without a break. One may relax when walking along the street, while having lunch or waiting for a visitor. Between business appointments, why not sit back with closed eyes? While dictating°, why not put your feet up on a stool or chair?

This ability to relax is one of the surest signs of health. But there is more to it. Relaxation is good for the mind and body: it is also a sign that one has an adequate philosophy of life. The man who can alternate° work and relaxation shows that he recognizes two worlds: the world as it is and the world he is working towards.

(Adapted from the *Monthly Letter* of the Royal Bank of Canada)

counsellor: adviser
tension: strain on the mind and nerves
relaxing: resting from work
centipede: worm with '100' legs
fatigue: tiredness
dictating: talking, while someone writes down what you say
alternate: change from (work to relaxation)

A centipede was happy quite
until a frog in fun
said: Pray°, which leg
comes after which?
he lay distracted° in a ditch°
considering how to run.

Pray: please tell me
distracted: not knowing what to do
ditch: channel beside the road

Stress° in class

Teachers should be paid a 'stress allowance' to compensate° them for the growing emotional and physical demands of their job, says a recent report. It claims that teachers suffer an unrelenting° pressure not realised by the rest of society.

'An effective comparison might be made with the actor, who is required to make an intense effort right through his performance. But in the case of the teacher the performance time is longer and he is expected to set up an interaction° with his "audience" which only a few actors have ever attempted.'

The 'stress allowance' could be justified for the same reasons as payments made to other professionals who do shift work° or are prepared to work at any time of the day or night, the report claims.

(*Yorkshire Post*)

stress: strain, pressure
compensate: repay, make up for
unrelenting: never stopping, pitiless
interaction: contact
shift work: usually done in factories, for a fixed period of time: one team works from, e.g. 06.00–14.00, then another team takes over

---

Unsocial-hours INDIGESTION?°

Relieve it with Triple Action Macleans.

Incorrect diet, rushed meals or anxiety° can all cause indigestion.

Don't suffer from indigestion, use Macleans' Triple Action formula. It will get you back to normal fast.

(Advertisement for Macleans)

indigestion: difficulty with the stomach after eating
anxiety: worry

DON'T KILL YOUR WIFE WITH WORK

Let ELECTRICITY DO IT

(Poster in Willesden)

(Denys Parsons, *Fun-tastic*)

DR. HANS SELYE M.D.

WORLD RENOWNED PROFESSOR, AUTHOR, LECTURER

PRESENTS:

Guidelines on how to live with stress, with sessions on:

- How to achieve your personal goals
- The imperative of goal-setting
- Conserving human energy by increasing productivity

7.00 pm, Wed. November 10, 1976, Constellation Hotel.

Registration at hotel $25.00.

(Toronto Globe & Mail)

guidelines: suggestions
stress: pressure
sessions: meetings
imperative: importance
conserving: saving

EVERY DAY BEFORE BREAKFAST AND AGAIN BEFORE DINNER, HALF A MILLION AMERICANS OF ALL AGES AND WALKS OF LIFE SIT IN A COMFORTABLE CHAIR AND CLOSE THEIR EYES. EFFORTLESSLY THEY SETTLE INTO DEEPER AND DEEPER STATES OF RELAXATION° WHILE THEIR MINDS REMAIN ALERT° WITH ENJOYMENT. THESE PEOPLE ARE ASTRONAUTS, SENATORS, CONGRESSMEN, A HIGH-RANKING CHINA EXPERT, PENTAGON GENERALS, NEW YORK JETS FOOTBALL PLAYERS, BASKETBALL CHAMPIONS, BROADWAY PLAYWRIGHTS, SCIENTISTS, ARTISTS, BUSINESSMEN, PROFESSORS, TEACHERS, HOUSEWIVES, STUDENTS AND CHILDREN. THEY ARE ALL PRACTITIONERS° OF TRANSCENDENTAL MEDITATION° (TM).

The TM program is neither a religion nor a philosophy. Rather it is a natural and effortless technique for improving all aspects of life, a way of putting life into high gear°, free of stress and tension, fatigue and anxiety. It may well be the most important thing ever to happen in your life – and this book is dedicated° to making the TM technique happen for you.

'A persuasive work with much to recommend it.'
The New York Times

(From inside cover of *TM, Discovering inner energy and overcoming stress*)

relaxation: resting (usually after hard work)
alert: wide awake
practitioners: people who use the method
transcendental meditation: (transcendental literally = 'going beyond') deep thought, concentration
(putting into) high gear: living at the 'right speed' (like a car engine)
dedicated to: written for the purpose of...

Fundamentals of world peace
PSYCHOLOGICAL HAPPINESS

Through the regular practice of the transcendental meditation° technique, psychological measurements show increased happiness, as indicated by:

- increased creativity, good-humour
- increased self-esteem°, self-assurance, self-acceptance and individuality
- increased liveliness of intellect°: improved intelligence and learning ability
- increased liveliness in academic studies; improved grades
- increased job satisfaction
- increased contentment°
- tendency to live in the present
- tendency to view man as essentially good
- reduced depression°
- reduced use of alcohol and cigarettes
- reduced anxiety°
- improved mental health
- more mature moral reasoning

(*The age of enlightenment*, Maharashi International University Press Publication, Switzerland)

transcendental meditation: deep thought and concentration
self-esteem: valuing oneself
intellect: brain
contentment: satisfaction
depression: unhappiness, dissatisfaction
anxiety: worry

The exercise for the control of the thoughts

One of the characteristics of the nervous person is that he lacks concentration°. His thoughts flit° from one thing to another and he is too much affected by what goes on around him.

Much nervous tiredness is due to the bad use of the power of thought. If we observe our thought life and our conversation it will be seen that we achieve very little truly-ordered thinking.

The exercise for gaining control of the thoughts consists in refusing, for a short time each day, to let all kinds of thoughts run through our mind.

We should concentrate with all our strength for five minutes a day – preferably before we begin the day's tasks – fixing our thoughts *on one simple object*, a familiar object such as a match, a pin, a lampshade or perhaps a pencil. Before doing so we should recall° each time the purpose of the exercise, which is *to bring order into our thinking*.

The aim is to banish° completely *all* other thoughts. Holding the object in the hand we look at it with concentration, observing every detail, and then, step by step, trace° the object back through its process of manufacture. When we have traced, for example a match, back to its source, the growing tree, we can then follow it mentally step by step back to its presence in our hand.

Five minutes of this exercise is enough. At first it will be difficult to make it last so long. One should not feel discouraged or irritated° when the mind wanders. This happens in all cases. It is only necessary to lead the mind calmly back to the exercise. What counts is the *effort* to achieve ordered thinking.

(Michael Rogers, *How to overcome nervousness*)

concentration: the power of fixing one's thoughts on one point
flit: jump
recall: remember
banish: drive away
trace: follow
irritated: annoyed by small things

Tense up° and live!

The myth° has got around that r-e-l-a-x-a-t-i-o-n always spells something good. Yet if you look up relax in the Oxford dictionary what it says is 'cause or allow to become loose or slack or limp . . .', none of which sounds particularly desirable or satisfying, does it? Do quite so many people need to relax as seem to think they do? Helping people to do it has become an industry involving many millions of pounds a year.

If you go to the doctor complaining that you feel unaccountably tired, depressed°, irritated° or dissatisfied, what you are almost certain to come away with is something 'to help you to relax'. Yet is it common knowledge in the medical profession that many 'depressed' patients are suffering not from too much going on in their lives but too little: their real need is not to be made less tense but to be given something worth being tense about.

We have become so accustomed to hearing the word 'tension' used pejoratively°, as the opposite of 'relaxation', that we tend to lose sight of the fact that, strictly speaking, a degree of tension is necessary. You have to be tense – sufficiently tense – to be motivated to write a book, paint a picture, learn a language, even to cook a meal. A totally 'relaxed' person would be a disaster, since he would lack any motivation to do anything.

The funny thing is that, secretly, we all know this. Yet because crude words like 'hard work', 'ambition' and 'goal' are out of fashion, we pretend to be above such earnest striving° (another unfashionable phrase).

If you analyse the 'relaxing holiday' people say they want, you usually find that what they really have in mind is skiing, dancing every night, having an adventure or 'getting to know the people', all of which require sustained° energy and skill. There is nothing like a holiday *really* doing nothing to make everyone thoroughly bad-tempered before the first week is out. Comparatively few people actually need to 'rest'; enormous numbers need to do something quite *different* from what they usually do, but equally, if not more, strenuous°. Abilities need to be used, at any age, or they go bad on you.

In our new frank° society the widespread, hidden vice° of

enjoying hard work surely cannot hope to remain a shameful secret for ever?

(Gillian Tindall, from *The Punch guide to good living*)

tense up: be more awake, more energetic
myth: (literally = folk tale or legend) false idea
depressed: deeply unhappy, often for no obvious reason
irritated: angry
pejoratively: in a bad sense
striving: trying (too) hard
sustained: continued
strenuous: requiring great effort
frank: honest
vice: bad habit, the opposite of 'virtue'

Whoever heard of ship-lag?°

These days businessmen do more travelling than ever before. And the time differences around the world can make you feel like you've done a day's work before breakfast. It's no wonder businessmen go grey and have heart attacks.

But don't despair°, if you're travelling to the States or Canada, Cunard have an attractive solution for the *weary*° traveller.

On 31 March, the Queen Elizabeth 2 begins her programme of 30 crossings between Southampton and New York. And if you've got a few days to spare, a cruise° on the QE2 makes a lot of sense.

If you want to relax before doing business or refresh yourself after it, the QE2 has everything you need from a sauna° to an excellent seven-course meal.

And if you *really* have to work, the QE2 has better facilities° than many offices – dictaphones, tape recorders, film and slide projectors and shorthand typists are all available. You can even book a conference room and hold meetings on board. Also, the ship-to-shore telephone will keep you in touch with anyone, anywhere in the world.

(Cunard Leisure, London)

ship-lag: a variant of the phrase 'jet-lag', the feeling ot tiredness caused by changing times and climates when flying round the world

despair: give up
weary: tired
cruise: voyage
sauna: (Finnish) dry steam bath
facilities: services

Pension point°

The problem, it is now clear, is to make *X* retire° at the age of 60. But how is *X* to be moved?

In this, as in so many other matters, modern science is not at a loss. The method depends essentially on air travel and the filling in of forms. Research has shown that complete exhaustion° in modern life results from a combination of these two activities. The high official who is given enough of each will very soon begin to talk of retirement°.

The technique is to lay before the great man the programme of a conference at Helsinki in June, a congress at Adelaide in July, and a convention at Ottawa in August, each lasting about three weeks. The essence of this technique is so to arrange matters that the conferences are held at places the maximum distance apart and in climates offering the sharpest contrast in heat and cold. There should be no possibility whatever of a restful sea voyage in any part of the programme.

It can safely be assumed that most flights will involve take-off at 2.50 a.m. Going one way around the world it is possible, and indeed customary, to have breakfast about three times. In the opposite direction the passengers will have nothing to eat for hours at a stretch, being finally offered a glass of sherry when on the point of collapse°. Most of the flight time will of course be spent in filling in various declarations° about currency and health. How much have you in dollars (US), pounds, francs, marks, guilders, yen, lire, and pounds (Australian); how much in traveller's cheques, postage stamps and postal orders? Where did you sleep last night and the night before that? (This last is an easy question for the air traveller is usually able to declare that he has not slept at all for the past week.) When were you born and what was your grandmother's maiden name? How many children have you and why? What will be the length of your stay and where? What is the object of your visit, if any? (As if by now you could even remember.) Have you had chicken-pox° and why not? Have you a visa for Patagonia and a re-entry permit for Hong Kong? The penalty° for making a false declaration is life imprisonment. Fasten your seat belts, please. We are about to land at Rangoon. Local time is 2.47 a.m. Outside temperature is 39°C. We shall stop here for approximately one hour. Breakfast will be served on the aircraft five hours after take-off. Thank you. (For what, in heaven's name?) No smoking, please.

Experiment has shown that an elderly man in a responsible position will soon be forced to retire if given sufficient air travel and sufficient forms.

(C. Northcote Parkinson, *Parkinson's law*)

pension point: the time when a person is old enough to stop work and retire, i.e. live off a pension
retire/retirement: stop work and live off a pension
exhaustion: extreme tiredness
collapse: loss of all strength of mind and body
declarations: forms, statements
chicken-pox: common children's disease
penalty: punishment

8 Down and out

Nobody loves you when you're down and out°

Once I lived the life of a millionaire
Spent all my money – I didn't care
Took all my friends out for a good time
Drank bootleg° liquor, champagne and wine.

Then I had a fall, oh so low
They didn't want me around their door
If I ever get my hands on a dollar again
I'm gonna keep it till those eagles° scream.

Nobody knows you
When you're down and out.
In my pocket – not one penny,
And for friends – I haven't any.

If I ever get back on my feet° again
I'll soon find all them long-lost friends,
Mighty strange without a doubt
Nobody wants you when you're down and out.

(Traditional blues song)

down and out: poor and lonely
bootleg: made and sold illegally
eagles: . . . the eagle, a bird, appears on the dollar bill; he means that he will hold on tight to his money!
get back on my feet: have money

I ain't got no home
I'm just a ramblin'° round
I'm just a wanderin' workin' man
I go from town to town
Police make it hard where I may go
And I ain't got no home in this world any more.

(Song by Woody Guthrie, from *Hard travellin'* by Kenneth Allsop)

ramblin': wandering

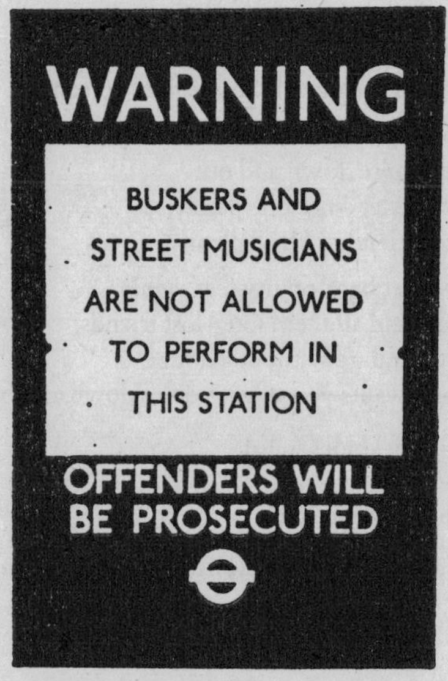

(Sign in London Underground)

buskers: beggars who sing or dance in the street
offenders: people who break the law
prosecuted: punished

Murder hunt after death of Old George

One of Holborn's cheekiest° characters is dead – murdered by four young thugs°.

Old George Humphreys boasted that he could make £20 an hour busking° with his mouth-organ outside Harrods°. His lack of musical talent never held him back: he won sympathy and pence from passers-by who felt sorry for the old man in dirty clothes.

George, a 70-year-old bachelor, was on his way to the cinema. On the bus, four youths argued with the conductor. In Regent Street the conductor told the youths to get off the no.6 bus. They got down without fuss° but then, in a moment of sudden anger, one of them threw a brick through the downstairs window of the bus. It hit George above the eye.

He was taken to hospital, treated, and released. But the next morning the staff° at Bruce House, where he lived, were anxious about his condition. They took him to St Thomas' hospital, where he died that night.

Mr Alfred Wynn, of the staff of Bruce House, said: 'Poor old George had been here for donkeys' years°. He used to go out busking, and boasted that he could make £20 in an hour playing to passers-by outside Harrods. I know it's true because I looked after his money. But he was a really terrible musician, who couldn't play a note right. He conned° tourists into thinking he was in real need by deliberately dressing in his oldest clothes.

He had a funny habit of spending his money on expensive cameras, rings and watches. But when he grew tired of them, he'd sell them for only a quarter of what he paid. When he died he had only £35 in the world. We hope the police catch the thugs who did this terrible thing.'

(*Holborn Guardian*)

cheekiest: 'naughtiest' and best-loved
thugs: tough young men, hooligans
busking: playing music for money in the streets
Harrods: an expensive London shop
fuss: trouble
staff: people in charge
for donkeys' years: (idiomatic) a very long time
conned: fooled

Better begging°

Since scientists get around to studying almost everything, it is not too surprising that a recent issue of the American journal *Science* looks at begging.

Psychologists° thought it would be interesting to see what made people give money to beggars.

The 'targets'° for the begging were simply asked for 10 cents (5p) without explanation by two male students. They approached a total of 79 different targets in either a 'submissive' manner (lowered head, dropped shoulders, the hand extended) or 'dominantly' (standing upright, no begging gesture, and looking the target in the eye). Some of the approaches were made in shabby° clothes, others in clothes unscientifically described as 'nice'. Some targets were eating, others were not.

Two girls were then added to the begging group. They were distinctly more successful than the men, but, as the targets included an approximately equal number of men and women, the explanation is not simple. It appears that women could successfully approach both women on their own and men, either in ones or twos. The 'dominant' approach was the more successful, and it was always better to beg from people who were eating. They often gave food as well as money.

Some people were best left alone°. A pair of women was a difficult target; a family even more so.

If a conclusion is to be drawn, it is not too kind about the givers' motives°. They will give, when alone, perhaps simply because of their loneliness; but a group – a family in particular – does not suffer from loneliness. To succeed in the art of begging, concentrate on individuals, preferably° while they are eating.

(*The Sunday Times*)

begging: asking other people for money
psychologists: scientists who study the reasons for our behaviour
targets: people to be asked
shabby: untidy, old
left alone: avoided
motives: reasons (for giving)
preferably: if possible

DUSSELDORF – A 38-year-old West German who learned to beg in four languages had nearly £20,000 in his bank account when he went on trial here for fraud°, Court sources said yesterday.

(Newspaper report)

raud: deceiving, cheating (in money matters)

HOT + COLD QUICK MEALS

FRIED SKATE + CHIPS	95p
FRIED PLAICE + CHIPS	95p
COD + CHIPS	85p
ENTRECOTE STEAK	£1.30
MIXED GRILL	£1.30
LAMB CHOP	60p
PORK CHOP	70p
CHICKEN BURGER + CHIPS	75p
HAMBURGER + CHIPS	65p
BEEFBURGER + CHIPS	55p
LIVER + CHIPS	70p
STEAK PIE + CHIPS	40p
PORK SAUSAGES + CHIPS	55p
STEAK CURRY + CHIPS	70p
STEAK CURRY	65p
EGGS + CHIPS	40p
HAM + CHIPS	75p
BEEF + CHIPS	75p
HAM SALAD	75p
BEEF SALAD	75p
CHEESE SALAD	45p
EGG SALAD	55p
MINUTE STEAK + CHIPS	75p

skate/ plaice/ cod: types of fish

Vagrants°–respectable and otherwise

Well, I'll tell you what happened to me in Birmingham. I was very much down and out. I was right in the gutter on the streets, and I met this gentleman. So he says, 'All you have to do,' he says, 'is go to the Salvation Army°.' So I says, 'Sir, you wouldn't get much in the Salvation Army.' 'Nonsense,' he says. 'I'll tell you what I'll do,' he says, 'I'll take you there. Come with me, I'll show you what the Salavation Army will do for you.' So, well, I said, 'Sir, you're making a bit of a mistake, I don't think they'll do anything for me.' 'Come,' he says, 'nonsense.' Of course, he was a gentleman, so right I goes down to the Salvation Army with him. So I goes down with him, and I says, 'Do you mind, Sir, walking behind me,' so that I could prove I was right. So I walks in and I says, 'Excuse me, could you give me a slice of bread and a cup of tea?' And the man in there says, 'Get out and beg it.' Well, I said, to tell you the truth, 'It's a bit late at night' (which it was). 'It's very hard to beg anything now, at this time at night.' Well, he says, 'We don't give nothing for nothing.' So I says, 'Thank you very much.' So I walks out and goes into an empty house the same night. Two policemen came in, they were doing their duty. I don't blame them for doing their duty. So the two of them came in and charged me with wandering and I got three months°. And that was Birmingham.

(Philip O'Connor, *Britain in the sixties: Vagrancy*)

vagrants: tramps, men who have no home
Salvation Army: an organization that looks after the poor, especially those living on the streets
three months: a prison sentence

I had a little beer shop
A man walked in
I asked him what he wanted.
A bottle of gin.
Where's your money?
In my pocket.
Where's your pocket?
I forgot it.
Please walk out.

(I. & P. Opie *The lore and language of schoolchildren*)

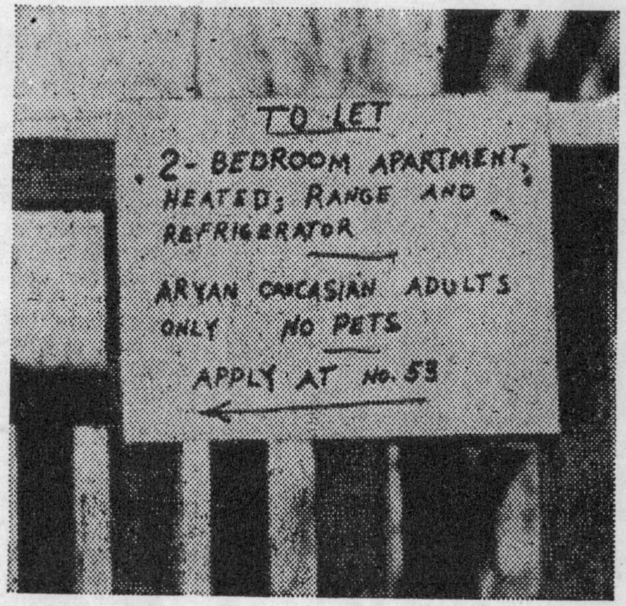

(*Toronto Globe & Mail*)

Aryan Caucasian: (in this context) White Christian
pets: animals kept in the home, e.g. dogs, cats, small birds

PARLIAMENT

The House met at 2 p.m.
Ministers were questioned.

New Democratic Party Leader Edward Broadbent: Mr Speaker, would the Minister also explain to the House why he dismissed° two practical proposals to increase the supply of low-cost housing and a tax reduction for low and medium income people° – two important steps to deal with unemployment – describing them as 'cold porridge'°, when the Government has not presented any porridge at all before 1977? Why does he reject these practical proposals out of hand°?

Manpower and Immigration Minister Jack Cullen: I did not say that it was cold porridge. I said that most of the things I read in the report presented by the honourable member on behalf of° his party seemed to me like warmed-over porridge.

(*Toronto Globe & Mail*)

dismissed: refused to accept
low and medium . . .: those who earn little or not much money
porridge: a breakfast food – always eaten hot!
out of hand: without considering them
on behalf of: for

Clowning around

A JUDGE ordered a man out of court yesterday ... for wearing a flashing° red clown's° nose.

The joker put on the battery-operated nose as he was about to give evidence. Judge Brian Grant angrily ordered him to be taken out.

The man was one of eight squatters°

who opposed an application by Brighton Council to turn them out of a house.

(*The Sun*)

flashing: with a light going off and on
clown: man in a circus who makes people laugh
squatters: people who move into an empty building and refuse to leave

---

IS LCK OF MNY MKING IT HRD TO LT YR FLT AT A GD RNT?

When you advertise your flat, don't sell it short by not describing it in full.

In The Guardian you can afford to spell out your message, even use a few adjectives.

GUARDIAN PERSONAL
One million readers for £1 a line.

(*The Guardian*)

Is Lck . . ., etc.: imitation of the special wording of an advertisement for a flat for sale (Is lack of money making it hard to let your flat at a good rent?)
sell it short: get too low a price for it

Readers are advised to take the necessary steps to protect their interests before parting with any money. It is preferable to conduct all transactions° through a solicitor° or established estate agent.

COME TODAY only, 27 Princess ct°, Queensway. Big lux.° 4 rm° 1 dble° bed & 2 sgl.° beds, kit.°, bath, CH°, own phone & TV, £39 pw°.

N15 Self-contained furnished flat. Next to Tube. Would suit 2 respectable people. References essential. £18 pw.

SW 17 S/c° 1 rm, k.° & b.° £23, 2 rm, k. & b. £29.

W2 comf.° dble rm. Ckg facs°, Tel., TV., serv.°, bkst°. Sgl. £15 dble £21 wkly°.

WIMBLEDON COMMON £12. Tiny room. Share bath, WC°.

(*Evening Standard*)

transactions: dealings
solicitor: lawyer
ct: court
lux:. luxurious
rm: room
dble: double
sgl.: single
kit., k.: kitchen
CH: central heating
pw: per week
S/c: self-contained
b.: bathroom
comf.: comfortable
serv.: service
ckg facs: cooking facilities (i.e. use of kitchen)
bkst: breakfast
wkly: weekly
WC: toilet, lavatory

Fairlawn Apartments

A temporary London home for visitors or families on the move, in warm, fully equipped service flats, sleeping 1–8, from £8.00 per day. Phone, linen, colour TV, baby-sitting and parking, buses. Tube nearby. Ready access° WEST END.

(*Observer Review*)

ready access: easy to reach

Complete home for sale. Two dble, one single bed, dining rm, wireless, television, carpets, lion, etc.

(*Portsmouth Evening News*)

(Denys Parsons, *Fun-tastic*)

*

DUNDAS $36,950

GOSH IT'S GREAT

Our modern family home, situated in a quiet street, on superb allotment°. Loads of accommodation° and minutes to school and transport.

DOBROYD POINT $79,950

MAGNIFICENT

Beautiful luxury family home, 4 double bedrooms, 2 ultra-modern bathrooms and huge kitchen. Provision° for inground° pool. Lock-up parking for 2 cars and boat. THIS PROPERTY MUST BE SEEN TO BE APPRECIATED.

Inspection by appointment only

(*Sydney Morning Herald*)

allotment: plot, piece of ground
loads of accommodation: plenty of room
provision: space
inground: sunk into the ground

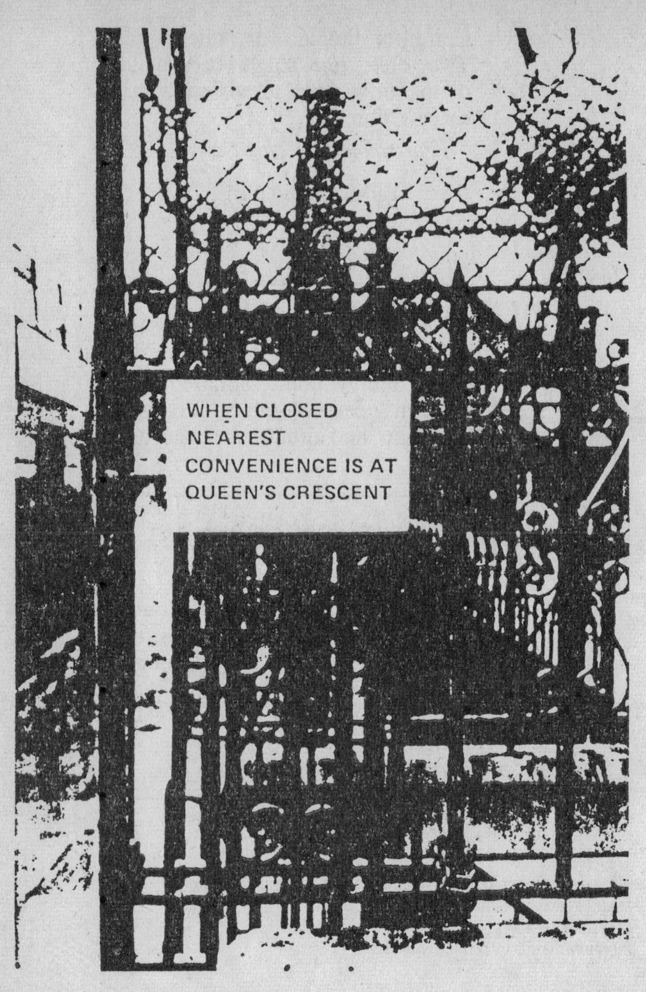

(Sign outside public lavatory near Hampstead)

and when open? . . .

Nowhere to call home

Tonight, thousands of young people, 2,000 of them girls, will be sleeping rough° on the streets of London. As the bitter cold of winter blows round them they will keep warm by walking, finally settling down in a shop doorway, a park bench or railway station for a fitful° sleep.

The story of 22-year-old Janice is typical. She had just arrived at a hostel° in North Kensington when I spoke to her. After months of sleeping rough she had spent her first night in a bed she could call her own. This is her story:

'My parents were separated. I still see my Dad sometimes, and he gives me a bit of money. But he's in lodgings° and he's got a tumour° on the brain.

My Mum died in 1975, so I had to leave home.

I had a baby, a little boy called Mark, so I lived in an unmarried mothers' home in Wimbledon for a while. But I couldn't stick° that, so I found a family to look after him and took a job making lampshades. I stayed with a friend for a couple of weeks, but she wasn't supposed to take lodgers° and when they found out I got chucked° out. No-one could help me, so I had to sleep rough.

It was early summer, but the nights were still cold. I'd° sleep in bus-shelters, shop doorways. But I'd only sleep for half an hour, then I'd hear a noise and wake up. The worst thing about being a girl sleeping out is all the men who approach you.

Sometimes I'd go to the police station and ask for a bed. When they did put me up° it was on a hard chair, and they kept waking me up and asking me if I was on drugs. People didn't believe I was sleeping rough because I looked so clean and tidy. I used to walk from Wallington to the public toilets in Sutton every day for a wash – I even used to wash my hair there. I kept all I needed in a plastic bag and used that as a pillow at night.

After five weeks of this I couldn't keep my job any longer. I spent my days walking round the shops, which was really depressing° because I didn't have any money to buy anything.

Then I moved in with a friend in a hostel, sleeping on the floor in her room. After six weeks I was sleeping out again, till I met a man who let me sleep in his car. Then

I stayed with friends. Next I went to a hostel in Cheam, but I was the youngest there and I couldn't stand it. Next day I came up to London to look for my brother. He wasn't there, but his friends suggested that I come to this hostel.

Now I've discovered that I'm expecting a baby again. I suppose I'll be in a mother-and-baby home somewhere, because I couldn't bear to have an abortion°. Then I don't know what will happen. I'll be back in the same old situation again, going round in the same circle.'

(Sandra Grant, *The Sunday Telegraph*)

sleeping rough: outside, in uncomfortable conditions
fitful: broken
hostel: cheap hotel, usually for students
lodgings: room(s) for which you pay money
tumour: growth
stick: bear, tolerate
lodgers: people who live in lodgings (see above)
chucked: thrown
I'd: I would = I used to
put (me) up: take (me) in for the night
depressing: making (her) unhappy
abortion: operation to get rid of a baby

The political education of Clarissa Forbes

A few weeks later Clarissa took a passage to England on an immigrant° ship, third class.

London was not all Clarissa expected it to be. True, there were fogs and days when it drizzled without stopping. But the fogs were not as thick or as yellow as she had been led to imagine° and there were many days when it did not rain. She lived in a bed-sitter° in an immigrant section of the city. Her landlord, a West Indian, charged her six pounds a week for it. It had peeling° wallpaper, a leaking ceiling and a stove that filled the room with smoke. She had no friends.

She was two months finding a job, as a ticket collector on the Underground. Week after week she sat outside her cubicle°, her hands stretched out to trap the stream of tickets. At nights she crept slowly back home, cooked supper and went to bed to the sound of trains that rattled past beneath her windows. Her landlord was sympathetic.

'I know how lonely it does get when you away° from home so long and all by yourself. But you get used to it in the end, like me.'

'I leave a good home to come to this,' Clarissa replied. 'My father is a councillor°. He would die if he was to see me living like this.'

'I been here ten years. Take me a long time to save up to buy this place. Ten years,' he repeated. 'Is warming° to meet a really nice local girl like you after such a long time. From the moment I set eyes on you I know you had class°. Real class. What you say your father is?'

'A councillor.'

'A councillor. Yes. You is a girl with real class.' He put his hand on her shoulder. Clarissa did not protest. 'I'm tired of these English girls.' He felt her hair. Still Clarissa did not protest. The landlord grew bolder. He swayed slightly as he bent low over her.

'You want to sleep with me?' Clarissa asked suddenly.

The landlord laughed, taken aback°. 'Real class,' he said.

'You want to sleep with me?'

'What a funny girl you is.'

'You want . . .'

'Yes, yes.'

And so Clarissa Forbes lost her virginity.

(Shiva Naipaul, *The political education of Clarissa Forbes*)

immigrant: person who leaves his own land to live and work in another country
led to imagine: told
bed-sitter: single room
peeling: coming off the wall
cubicle: small 'box'
when you away: (West Indian dialect) when you're away (both Clarissa and the Landlord speak in West Indian English)
councillor: member of the town council, an important man
is warming: (West Indian) it's pleasant
(had) class: were well brought up
taken aback: shocked, surprised

PRIVATE
RIGHT OF WAY
NO PARKING
NO RUBBISH

NO GOODS OR ARTICLE
MAY BE PLACED IN
FRONT OF THIS GATE
BY ORDER
G.A.F.SUTTON

NOTICE
NO OBSTRUCTION OF
ANY DESCRIPTION TO BE
LEFT IN THIS
ENTRANCE
Trespassers will be Prosecuted

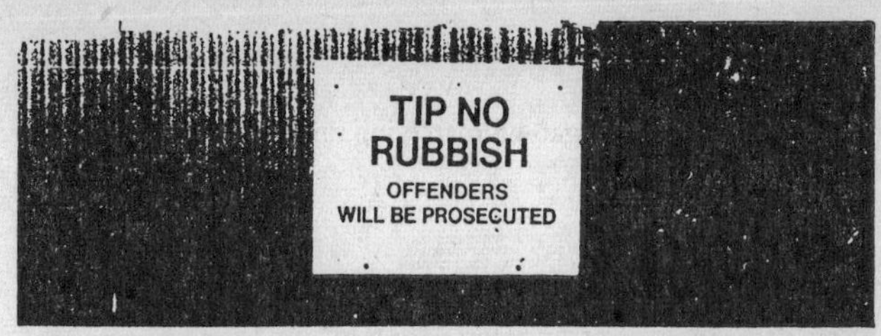

ELECTRICITY SUPPLY
PLEASE LEAVE ACCESS
TO THESE GATES AT
ALL TIMES

trespassers: people who enter buildings or property when they are not allowed to
prosecuted: taken to court

from **Heat and Dust**

[The author finds a beggar-woman lying on a heap of rubbish in a town in India.]

15 June

There is an alley° behind our house where our washerman lives. A few days ago I took some clothes to him, and I can't be sure of this but I think she may have been lying there at the time. The trouble is, one is so used to her that one tends not to see her. But I definitely noticed her when I went back to fetch the clothes. There was something about the way she was lying there that drew my attention. The lane ends in a piece of land where the municipality° have put up a concrete refuse° dump°, but most people see no point in throwing their refuse into the concrete enclosure, so that it lies around, forming a little mound°. The reason why I noticed the beggar woman was because she was lying on the edge of this mound of refuse. I thought at first she was dead, but realised this could not be since no one else seemed concerned.

Later I wondered what had happened to me – that I had not even bothered to go close to see whether she was alive or dead. I told Inder Lal about her, but he was busy getting ready to leave for his office. I wanted him to come with me to see her so I followed him when he started off. He was wheeling his bicycle with his tiffin carrier° tied to the handlebar. Although he was very reluctant°, I persuaded him to enter the alley with me. I saw at once that she was still there. We stopped to look at her from a distance. 'Is she alive?' I asked him. He didn't know and was not inclined° to investigate; anyway, it was time for him to go, he could not be late at the office. I decided I had to see. I stepped closer – Inder Lal cried 'No, don't!' and even rang the bell of his bicycle as a warning. I went up to the refuse dump. I stood over the beggar woman: her eyes were open, she was groaning°, she was alive. There was a terrible smell and a cluster of flies. I looked down and saw a thin stream of excrement° trickling out of her. My first thought was for Inder Lal: I made gestures to him to go away, go to his office. I was glad he had remained at a distance. I gestured more wildly and was relieved when he turned away – clean in his much washed clothes with his freshly cooked food in his tiffin carrier. I walked away. The washerman could be seen through the doorway eating his food in the courtyard. I could not disturb him. In fact, I felt I could not disturb or go near anyone. For the first time I understood – I *felt* – the Hindu fear of pollution°. I went home and bathed, washing myself over and over again. I was afraid. Pollution – infection – seemed everywhere; those flies could easily have carried it from her to me.

(Ruth Prawer Jhabvala, *Heat and dust*)

alley: small street
municipality: town council
refuse: rubbish
dump: pile
mound: pile
tiffin carrier: food tin
reluctant: unwilling
inclined: willing
groaning: making sounds of pain
excrement: waste matter from the body
pollution: becoming unclean

London's mini-house

In these days of high-rise flats and towering office blocks, one is likely to overlook° buildings which come at the other end of the scale°. This is certainly the case with a house a little way along Bayswater Road from Marble Arch which is squeezed between two much larger buildings. It dates from 1806 and consists of two 10-metre passages, one above the other, and not more than 1.25 metres wide. There is no gas, electricity, bathroom or lavatory, and when an author occupied it for a time while writing a book, he was only just able to squeeze past his bed. His portable° heater had to be placed exactly half-way between the walls to avoid scorching° them.

(J. Hart, 'London oddities', London Transport brochure)

overlook: not notice
at the other end . . . : very small buildings
portable: which can be carried
scorching: burning the surface

(Street signs near Covent Garden)

GLC: Greater London Council. Covent Garden used to be London's main market. The Council, however, decided to move it.

The City Machine*

'When our ancestors° came to this world,' said Ryne, 'one group wanted to try to live in the open as Earth people had. The other wanted to be protected as they had been in the ship° that brought them here. It was this group that built the City. The others struggled for a time against the terrible weather of the Out and against the wild animals. Then they disappeared, but we don't know whether they died or moved to a better part of the planet°.

'Go on,' said the Coordinator.

'The original City was on one level, but as time passed two social groups developed – those who laboured and those who managed. They lived side by side until the Highs came from space. They had a higher technology and used it to gain control of the City. When they had complete control, they built a new

City on top of the old, a City with three levels instead of one. The Highs put the workers on the lowest level, the managers above them, and themselves at the top.'

'That sounds like a lesson you learned from your grandfather,' the Coordinator said. 'I'm not going to waste time arguing about the truth of it. It's enough for you to remember that whatever you once were, now you're an Upper.'

He moved closer to Ryne. 'And as an Upper you own a share in the City. You're part of it. The City lives to protect us. It keeps away the terrors and dangers and discomforts of the Out, and it feeds and clothes us. It provides the air we breathe, the water we require, the food we need. It is never too warm nor too cold. It takes little from us physically because our bodies never need to adjust° to changes in climate.'

He saw that he was stepping beyond the limits of Ryne's understanding. 'Climate – changes in weather. Something none of us have ever known except through the old films that show Earth and the planets our ancestors colonized in the early days of space exploration.

(Louis Trimble, *The city machine*)

ancestors: people who lived before us, of our own race or nation
ship: space ship, rocket
planet: large star
adjust: change, get used to

*Editorial note: This passage is taken from a science fiction story (dealing with recent or imagined scientific discoveries and advances).

9 Anything new?

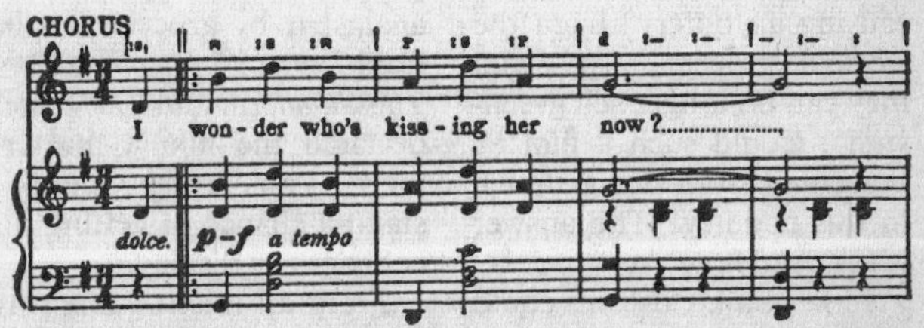

I wonder who's kissing her now
I wonder who's teaching her how
I wonder who's looking into her eyes
breathing sighs
telling lies
I wonder who's buying the wine
for lips that I used to call mine
I wonder if she
ever tells him of me
I wonder who's kissing her now

(Hough, Adams, Howard, as sung by Ray Charles)

The protection business

Let us imagine that Hans von Trupp, a noted director, makes a film about cabbages which suggests that all vegetables are pederasts°, thus causing an outcry° from the world's grocers who claim they can no longer sell greenstuff°. Could such a film be prevented from being shown in this country? The answer is yes. And how°.

First of all, Customs could seize the offending film and send it straight back to H. von Trupp, Bavaria. Secondly, the British Board of Film Censors° could refuse to give it a certificate. And thirdly, if neither Customs nor the Board of Censors cared a damn about cabbages, local authorities would step in and ban the film.

But that isn't all. Various parts of the law could be used against it by grocers. To be frank, even if *The Guardian*, *The Standard*, and *The Times* declared the film a masterpiece, Von Trupp wouldn't stand a chance of getting his cabbages on display.

From all this it can easily be seen that film censorship in this country is in an appalling° mess, and that the muddle° clearly favours those who want things banned rather than those who don't. No other art form finds itself so threatened.

(*The Guardian*)

pederast: homosexual, person who is sexually interested only by people of his or her own sex
outcry: protest
greenstuff: vegetables
and how: (colloquial) definitely!
Censors: inspectors, who decide whether a film may or may not be shown
appalling: terrible
muddle: confusion

Now, that's a *story*!

(Howard has written a book which he hopes will be made into a film by the famous director, Bill Saltman. Saltman is taking a shower while talking to Howard . . .)

Bill Saltman's head appears round the door, with fingers of wet hair hanging over his leathery brown forehead.

'So what's the story, Howard?' he demands.

'Well,' says Howard, jumping up, and beginning to walk up and down, 'it's the story of this society, where everyone begins to get more and more aware of its real nature, and . . .'

'In two words, Howard. I'm standing here with water running off me.'

'Well, people begin to make a structural analysis . . .'

'Hold it. I'll put some clothes on.' When he comes back he is wearing a shirt and a pair of socks held up by suspenders. I'll tell you what a story is, Howard,' he says. 'A story is when something happens. A story is when someone's trying to do something, and someone's trying to stop him. So, wham, there's a fight on.'

'Yes, well . . .'

'A story is when this McTavish you have in the book – we'll have to change that name, by the way . . .'

'It's McKechnie.'

'That's worse. A story is when McTavish wants to build a better world for everyone – just like you have it in the book, I don't want to change anything – and the local hoods° jump on him. Or his wife, even – she turns against him. How about that, Howard? His wife, his own wife! That could be good. "Oh God, Mary!" says McPherson, "Oh God, Mary!" – his voice is breaking with emotion – "Oh God, Mary, I don't want our kids to grow up in a world like this, with man an enemy to man. I want a decent world where a man can stand on his own two feet, etcetera, etcetera, etcetera°." '

'Yes, well . . .'

'Listen, Howard. And Mary says, "Don't make trouble, Lester! You'll lose your job! Haven't we always been happy together the way we are? You testify° before the Commission tomorrow and I take the kids and go home to mother in Milwaukee." Now, that's a *story*, Howard!'

'But isn't this going to lead to violence, and, and . . .'

The doorbell rings.

'Let her in, Howard, while I put my pants on. I'll see you tomorrow, at twelve o'clock, and maybe we can get in an hour's work before lunch.'

So this is how it's going to be, thinks Howard, as he rides down in the lift again. An exhilarating° struggle between the intellectuality° of his concept and the strong vulgarity° of Bill Saltman's.

(Michael Frayn, *Sweet dreams*)

hoods: (slang) hoodlums, i.e. tough men, gangsters
etcetera: and so on; Saltman means 'you know the kind of speech I'm thinking of'
testify: give evidence in court
exhilarating: exciting
intellectuality: lack of simplicity
vulgarity: rudeness

Some day my prince will crawl

> 'A group of the women's liberation movement on Merseyside is rewriting fairy tales, in which men and women will be shown to have equal opportunities.' (*The Guardian*)

. . . so Little Red Riding Hood took off her cloak, but when she climbed up on the bed she was astonished to see how her grandmother looked in her nightgown.

'Grandmother dear! she exclaimed, 'what big arms you have!'

'All the better to hug you with, my child!'

'Grandmother dear, what big ears you have!'

'All the better to hear you with, my child!'

'Grandmother dear, what big eyes you have!'

'All the better to see you with, my child!'

'Grandmother dear, what big teeth you have!'

'All the better to eat you with, my child!'

With these words, the wicked Wolf leapt upon Little Red Riding Hood, and stopped a short right to the jaw°.

'HAI!°' cried Little Red Riding Hood, giving a textbook karate° jab to the ribs that brought the Wolf to its knees.

'AKACHO!' screamed Little Red Riding Hood, following up with a neck chop°, a double finger eye-prod, and a reverse groin kick.

The Wolf coughed, once, and expired° on the rug.

At that moment, the door of the little house flew open, and the woodchopper burst in, brandishing° his axe.

'Little Red Riding Hood!' he cried, 'are you all right?'

'No thanks to you!' snapped Little Red Riding Hood, snatching the axe from him, breaking it across her knee, and tossing it into the corner. 'And while you're at it, wash the dishes!'

With which she cracked her knuckles° and strode out into the forest, slamming the door behind her.

(Alan Coren, *The sanity inspector*)

stopped . . . jaw: got a punch in the face (as in boxing)
HAI: (Japanese) cry, given when attacking
karate: (Japanese) special fighting techniques used mostly for self-defence
neck chop, etc.: different kinds of blows
expired: died
brandishing: waving
knuckles: finger joints

My holiday snaps used to keep my friends amused for hours

No matter how much trouble I took with them, my holiday photographs always came out wrong.

Some would be too light, others too dark, out of focus° or crooked°.

And if I took pictures of people, I'd somehow always manage to cut off vital parts of their anatomy°.

They'd lose arms, legs, even heads. My friends started to call me Henry° because I cut off so many heads. And the awful thing was, I thought my pictures were bad because I was a bad photographer.

Then, one day, one of my friends took me aside. 'Have you ever thought,' he said, 'that maybe what's wrong with your pictures isn't you but your camera?'

(Advertisement for Olympus cameras)

snaps: photographs
out of focus: not clear
crooked: not straight
anatomy: body
Henry: after King Henry the Eighth, who killed most of his six wives by having their heads chopped off

The Blues

'The blues ain't nothin',' Duke Ellington once observed, 'but a dark cloud markin' time°'.

Part of the difficulty in identifying the blues lies in the variety of meanings attached to the word. Webster's Dictionary begins by defining blues as 'low spirits, mental depression,' with despondency° and melancholy° listed as synonyms°. The second definition is: 'A song sung or composed in a style originating among American Negroes, characterized by the use of three line stanzas° in which the words of the second line repeat the first, expressing a sense of longing or melancholy . . .'

It all sounds very cut and dried°. The trouble is that no dictionary, no printed words on a sheet of paper, can ever convey° to any reader the immense range of emotions, concepts, and styles of musical tempos and moods to which the word can justifiably be applied.

(Leonard Feather, *The history of the blues*)

markin' time: staying in the same place
despondency, melancholy: feeling sad
synonyms: words of the same meaning
stanzas: verses
cut and dried: uninteresting, scientific
convey: explain

When prohibition° hit Southern Comfort New Orleans discovered The Blues

In 1920 the US Government, for reasons best known to itself, decided that nobody should drink anything stronger than coffee.

Which was especially tough on the citizens of New Orleans.

Not because their coffee was particularly bad, but because their alternative° was particularly good.

It was called Southern Comfort.

And shortly after it disappeared, a new style of music became popular. It was called The Blues.

All over New Orleans, gravel°-voiced gentlemen began to sing of their troubles.

The source of much of their distress° was the lack of Southern Comfort. This had been invented some 50 years earlier by a New Orleans man who despaired of finding any liquor that didn't feel like sandpaper° as it went down.

So it is hardly surprising that when Southern Comfort once again became available in 1933, The Blues gradually began to fade away.

Or at least, it could be the reason why the gravel-voiced gentlemen were never quite so gravel-voiced again.

(Southern Comfort Corporation)

prohibition: total ban by the Government on the sale of alcohol
alternative: choice
gravel: small hard stones, often used for paths and roads
distress: unhappiness
sandpaper: special rough paper used for making wood smooth

The blues – the song of the walking wounded

Jazz is the art of surprise, producing always the sudden and unexpected. But the blues is something else. Jazz has been developed into one of those intellectual art forms that scares people away. The blues can be faked°. It is faked more today than ever before. But it is emotional song and even the finest of blues singers cannot always possess true emotions, the real grief° which is at the heart, in the soul.

Of course, I had heard the blues all my life. I had heard it all as a teenage jazz fan in America, travelling long distances to sit, perfectly still, listening with religious reverence° to the great progressive jazzmen of the day. But I was never moved by the blues until I was a young soldier, marching along one long, desperately hot afternoon under a south Texas sun. We were marching four abreast°, rifles slung°, singing as we swung along.

An officer marched at the head of us. He did not sing. God how we hated them, the officers. We all hated them. The officer was only there for show. Like a fancy motor car radiator cap°. Suddenly on our left there appeared this ghostly° vision. All in white. Pure white. It was men. A prison work-gang. All black men dressed in white. They sang as they worked. They were not in chains, but men on horseback watched over them.

The men on horseback were unmoved, bored by the singing of the prison work-gang. Maybe they heard too much of it. But the beauty of their singing stirred us. We stopped singing our own silly song as we drew near them. Many of us were university graduates. Being soldiers in the infantry was the closest we would ever come, with luck, to joining the down-trodden° of the earth.

The prison gang were singing some work-song. We all, all of us felt it; knew the feeling of the song for we were prisoners too and knew something at least of the longing that went into that song.

Without ever stopping their work the black convict gang saw us. The scene, the beauty of their singing, of these black men who were the grandsons of kidnapped° African men and women, the descendants of slaves, burned our eyes. The blues, sung like this, in the condition of penal servitude° which was its true roots, and set against this dusty lonesome Southern backdrop°, was the real thing. All the concerts, jazz sessions and recordings I had listened to again and again – none of it was like this.

(Stanley Reynolds, *Radio Times North*)

faked: falsely imitated, played without real feeling
grief: deep sorrow
reverence: respect
abreast: in line, side by side
rifles slung: guns on our shoulders
radiator cap: a small ornament in the front of the car
ghostly: unreal
down-trodden: the poorest and weakest
kidnapped: taken by force
penal servitude: prison with hard labour
backdrop: setting

This day as he leaned against a lamppost at the corner of One Hundred and Third Street and San Pedro, a tall handsome young black man walked up to him and said, 'Are you the kid that plays cello°? Remember me? I'm Buddy Collette.' He introduced the boys with him, who were all laughing and grinning though Charles failed to see anything funny.

'How'd you like to make bread° and wear the sharpest° clothes in the latest styles?' Buddy asked. 'Look at yourself. You dress like a hobo°.'

'I don't dig° clothes any more.'

'How'd you like to have the finest chicks° in town?'

Charles said he wouldn't mind that at all.

'All right, join the Union,' Buddy said. 'Get yourself a bass° and we'll put you in our Union swing band. We can use you.'

'Get a *bass*?'

'That's right. You're black. You'll never make it in classical music no matter how good you are. You want to play, you gotta play a *Negro* instrument. You can't slap° a cello, so you gotta learn to *slap that bass*, Charlie!'

Charlie liked the way Buddy talked and admired his adult manner and extreme good looks so he went home and discussed it with his father, explaining he had a chance to make a lot of money if he traded his cello for a bass. His parents, as usual not really knowing but hoping for the best, agreed to help.

(Charles Mingus, *Beneath the underdog*)

cello: stringed instrument, mostly used in classical music
bread: (slang) money
sharpest: (slang) smartest
hobo: tramp
dig: (slang) like
chicks: (slang) girls
bass: stringed instrument, larger than the cello, used in both jazz and classical music
slap: (slang) play

How punk° became a four-letter word°

Malcolm McLaren, young manager of the Sex Pistols rock group, munched at a sausage sandwich in a North London café, cleared his throat, and delivered: 'Punk rock players are nearly all ex-Borstal° or unemployed lads. They are England's next generation and we will learn to be proud of them.'

At a neighbouring table a little earlier, four punk rock musicians had drunk tea out of glass cups. Their hair was close-cropped, sometimes almost shaved, sometimes dyed a vivid orange. Safety-pins, old bicycle chains, razor blades served as jewellery. Clothes were torn or odd. Teeth seemed a little green.

Punk rock has arrived so quickly that there's not even broad agreement about what to call it. 'High energy rock,' say the Sex Pistols. 'New wave rock,' say the Damned. 'Nasty kid rock,' says a critic. But all are agreed that punk rock is played almost exclusively by working-class kids, that it has come from nothing in the last 12 months, and is doing its job by inflaming° the good, the decent and the hard-working. They also agree that punk-rock musicians have a lot in common: outside music they'd be dead-end° kids.

Malcolm McLaren, an ex-art student, said: 'They are part of this generation which has come out of school with no future, no jobs, no chance to buy decent clothes because they have no money, and only a lot of unemployment ahead of them.'

The punk-rock musicians produced their pedigree°. Johnny Rotten of the Pistols: 'Unemployed and bored to death'. David Vanium of the Damned: 'I had a job as a gravedigger for a year.' Two other Damned musicians met while employed as lavatory attendants at Croydon.

In contrast to the public rage, experienced observers of rock music are by no means willing to write off° punk rock. Laurie Taylor, Professor of Sociology, said: 'Rock music always starts off with something outrageous°. But in a very short time it becomes refined and acceptable.' Memories of past outbursts about rock groups are quoted by protectors of punk rock. They remind us of the days when television cameras would not show us Elvis Presley's lower limbs when he sang, the days when the Rolling Stones were considered dangerous and degenerate°. As one man said: 'In 10 years or so, we'll be hearing the Sex Pistols on "These you have loved"°.'

(Jeremy Bugler, *The Observer*)

punk (rock): pop music (punk, literally, means rotten, worthless)
four-letter word: rude
ex-Borstal: coming from an institution (Borstal) for young criminals
inflaming: making angry
dead-end: hopeless
pedigree: personal history, usually to prove noble origins in both people and animals
write off: dismiss as worthless
outrageous: shocking
degenerate: immoral
"Those you have loved": programme of favourite songs of the past

The Sex Pistols

A few months ago I was guest performer on the Granada TV show 'So It Goes', in which the Sex Pistols made their television debut°. So noxious° was their behaviour during rehearsals that they were very nearly removed from the show. This was the first time in history that a pop group had ever tried to bite the hand that fed it before it had been fed°.

During the recording, the task of keeping the little bastards under control was given to me. With the aid of a radio microphone I was able to shout them down, but it was a near thing°. The Sex Pistols are not long on° vocabulary, but they make up for it by being short on temper. They attacked everything around them and had difficulty in being polite even to each other. Their leader, a foul-mouthed ball of acne° calling himself something like Kenny Frightful, kept trying to kick himself in the stomach.

My evening with the Sex Pistols left me feeling sad and old. This was what the pop dream had finally come to. One had already grown used to pop performers after the release of the first Elvis Presley singles° who dressed up in silly clothes and pretended to be horrible. But here were performers born after the release of the first Beatles singles who were dressing up in silly clothes and really *were* horrible.

(Clive James, *The Observer*)

debut: start
noxious: unbearable
bite the hand. . . fed: from the saying 'Never bite the hand that feeds you' i.e. do not be ungrateful to the person who gives you your work and pays you
a near thing: (in this sense) difficult
not long on (vocabulary): they do not use many words
acne: skin disease on the face
singles: short records

So respectable, the managing director who's behind the four-letter punks on disc

The wave of protest over punk rock and the Sex Pistols reached the stockbroker belt° yesterday.

In Gerrard's Cross, a haven° of respectability in leafy Buckinghamshire, there was strong condemnation° of people who profit from the new cult°.

This is where Mr Leslie Hill has his home. Mr Hill, as managing director of EMI records, approved the £40,000 contract that the Sex Pistols have signed with his company.

Mr Hill's neighbours did not think much of him for it. 'The whole thing is pretty disgusting,' said Mr Ronald Barton. 'I am very much against this playing to the lowest standards, and I think that the responsibility for this must rest with the head of the record company.' Another neighbour, Mrs Livermore, said: 'The whole thing is absolutely sick and disgusting, and I believe that the people running the television and record companies have a duty to set standards of decency.'

(*Daily Mail*)

stockbroker belt: area where the rich live
haven: safe place
condemnation: criticism, sharp attack
cult: fashion, craze

'Last Supper°' set in a pub

The Last Supper as the Scottish artist Stewart Johnson sees it: the setting is in a Glasgow bar, the disciples° are in modern dress, several wearing Celtic° and Rangers° scarves, and a card game with coins (30 pieces of silver) is in progress.

Stewart Johnson, 38, painted the Last Supper scene for his own one-man show. 'It was never painted to be controversial,°' he said. 'The point is: all those fishermen at the Last Supper, I mean, they had to be tough and rough fishermen. So I thought the working men in Glasgow could just as easily be similar looking characters.'

The painting shows Judas as surreptitiously° sliding out of the pub door, and the cross is formed by a window frame.

(*Yorkshire Post*)

the Last Supper: Christ's last meeting with his closest followers (disciples); there are many pictures of this scene, including one by Leonardo da Vinci
disciples: followers
Celtic, Rangers: well-known Scottish football clubs
controversial: shocking
surreptitiously: secretly

NAIROBI – A man evidently under the influence of alcohol walked into St Emmanuel's Church, near Embu, Kenya, and asked the Bishop of Mount Kenya to crucify° him.

(Newspaper report)

crucify: nail to a large wooden cross (this is how Jesus Christ died)

Art folds up

A blank white sheet of paper with a crease° in it – given the title of 'Folded Paper' – has been included in the Thamesdown Borough Council's progressive art gallery in Swindon. The 45-cm-square piece of paper has been loaned free of charge from a private collection. It was 'created' by artist Sol Lewitt in July 1973.

(*The Observer*)

crease: fold

10 One for the road

How do you give a good party?

Mix your guests but not your drinks.
(Olga Deterding)

*

Have good food, good wine, and no bores.
(Duchess of Beford)

(*Observer Magazine*)

Those fish were only drunk

BELGRADE – Thousands of fish believed to have been poisoned by industrial waste in the Jadar River have suddenly recovered, to the delight of anglers°. They were only drunk.

Experts said a factory making alcoholic drinks had released some brandy into the river, causing many fish to float on the surface with strange unfishlike looks.

(Newspaper report)

anglers: fishermen

HOW TO MIX A POLAR BEAR

On the ice before you looms° a white shape. It is the Smirnoff Polar Bear, a species known for its conviviality°.

But you need not tread° the tundra° to track down° this delightful creature. Just follow the simple directions and a Polar Bear will appear in your glass.

To make a Polar Bear, pour Smirnoff into a glass with ice, add twice as much milk and a drop of maple syrup°. Stir°.

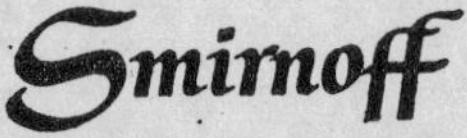

(Advertisement for Smirnoff Vodka)

looms: appears
conviviality: sociability, friendliness
tread: walk across
tndra: frozen land in the north
track down: find
maple syrup: thick, sweet juice, rather like honey
stir: mix

Vodka neat° – a comrade's road to ruin

A few years ago, over the photographs of drunkards, hooligans° and idlers°, the members of the People's Patrol used to write: 'We are not taking this lot into communism with us.' They hoped that public humiliation° would turn so-called difficult youths into responsible adults, but they were to be disappointed. Difficult youths became difficult adults and excessive drinking continues to be a problem in the Soviet Union.

In 1970, *Pravda* admitted that more than half of all law-breaking was done under the influence of drink; by 1974 the figure had risen to three quarters. Wife-beating after heavy drinking is now the most frequently recorded complaint in the divorce courts. In the summer, hundreds of Soviet citizens are said to drown 'in mysterious circumstances while bathing'. In fact, the workers' paper *Trud* had to warn: 'People who drink like fishes can no longer swim like fishes.'

It seems that the only weapon left in the fight against excessive drinking is public opinion. As soon as friends and neighbours and colleagues start to frown upon° those who drink, then the practice may decline°.

The dreaded sobering up° centres are playing their part in this respect. Here recordings are taken of those under the influence of drink. When sober, Citizen Vladimir has to listen to his ramblings° before being handed over to his family or work colleagues. Such a public humiliation brings a few to their senses and is said to be more successful than increased fines or refusing sickness benefit for those who are off work because of drinking.

Perhaps the People's Patrol was right in its approach. Instead of seeing pictures of Good Citizens in every factory and city centre, we shall soon see photographs of the Baddies under the words: 'We are not taking this lot into communism with us.'

(*The Guardian Weekly*)

neat: straight, without water or ice
hooligans: small criminals
idlers: lazy persons
humiliation: shame
frown upon: disapprove (of)
decline: get less
sobering up: returning to 'normal'
ramblings: senseless talking while drunk

Is drinking good for you?

A drop of what you fancy° tastes good, feels good. And, thankfully, it really DOES do you good.

Live it up and live longer – that's the view of some top American doctors who were asked what they thought about the evils of drink. Evil? Not a bit of it. They all agreed that drink in moderation° is often a blessing in disguise°. They said it had helped hundreds of their patients to recover and stopped thousands more from ever becoming patients at all.

In his book, *Drink to your health*, Junius Adams writes: 'Moderate drinkers live longer and have a lower rate of reported heart attacks than former drinkers or teetotallers°.'

Take the case of the 94 pairs of brothers whose drinking habits were measured. One brother in each pair was a drinker, the other wasn't. All the drinkers lived longer than their non-drinking brothers. The survey was stopped only when the last of the non-drinkers died.

(*The Sunday Times*)

fancy: enjoy, feel like
(in) moderation: in reasonable amounts
a blessing in disguise: (idiomatic) an advantage or piece of luck, although it does not appear to be one
teetotaller: person who never drinks alcohol

Turn to the friend in your fridge

It is important at all times of the year to keep the fridge well stocked° with milk, particularly during the summer, when the children are home from school.

Milk can be regarded as the friend in your fridge for several very good reasons:

- it is a nourishing° food
- it is a refreshing food
- it is good value for money
- it can be used for a wide variety of dishes and drinks
- every drop can be used

Can you think of any other food for which all these claims can be made?

Milk is conveniently delivered to your door. It arrives in a clear glass bottle so that you can see exactly what you are buying. And milkmen, while delivering fresh supplies, also collect the 'empties' so that they do not clutter up° the kitchen.

(Advertisement for The Milk Board, *The Guardian*)

stocked: supplied
nourishing: giving strength and energy
clutter up: lie in the way

Not enough puff

Lady driver Ann Bishop couldn't blow hard enough for the satisfaction of police when she was pulled up° in the West End and asked to take a breath test°.

And Miss Bishop did not manage to inflate° the bag fully in a second attempt at the police station.

Police Inspector Hill said this when Miss Bishop admitted driving with an excess° of alcohol in her blood. The Inspector said she refused to give a blood sample at the station and the doctor was told to leave. She then agreed to give blood and the doctor was called again, at double expense to the police.

She had nothing to say about the offence° but claimed she had been ill-treated by the police and dragged into their car. 'I was stopped several times that week and it was getting on my nerves,' she said.

(*Camden Chronicle*)

pulled up: made to stop
breath test: blowing into a special bag to show if you have been drinking
inflate: blow up
excess: too much
offence: crime

IT'S CRIMINAL THE WAY SOME PEOPLE DRINK AND DRIVE

Most people in this country drink and drive. You are probably one of them. If you're like most others, you stay within what you think is the legal limit when you're driving. Or you don't drink.

Alcohol is associated with approximately 40 % of all traffic deaths
Yet, there may have been times when you were impaired° without knowing it. So, you'd had only a few drinks; but it takes only a few°. You're still impaired. If you're taking a prescription°, or something you bought in a drugstore for an ache or pain the combined effect with alcohol could impair your driving ability considerably. You know you can't be too careful.

However, there are some people who don't seem to care
In fact, they think disregarding° the law is something to be proud of. 'You should have seen me last night. I was so drunk, I couldn't walk, I had to drive.' The tragedy is that persons who have said that, could have killed themselves and others; yet their friends thought it was funny. Instead of laughing at that kind of behaviour, it's time to speak out against it. Support tough° laws.

Tell people who have been drinking not to drive
It isn't easy. Some people don't like being told. But, if you have the courage of your convictions°, others will too. If you're not sure what to say, cut this out and talk about it with someone else. If you have any comments, we'd like to hear from you. We believe that if enough people talk about the problems, we're that much closer to solving them.

(Dialogue on drinking, Health & Welfare, Canada)

impaired: not in full control of yourself
it only takes a few: you don't need many drinks
prescription: medicine (for which a paper from the doctor is needed)
disregarding: paying no attention to
tough: severe
the courage . . .: (idiomatic) ready to fight for your beliefs

Drinking drivers

It is all very well° for you to urge° the Government to introduce stricter drink-and-drive laws; but have you considered that it is already impossible for the drinking man who lives in the country, and in other places where there is no public transport, to go out to dinner either with friends or to a restaurant without breaking the law? Surely it is wrong for people to have to break the law week after week or restrict° their social lives to almost nothing?

Surely a better solution would be this: anyone who has drunk more than two pints of beer, or the same amount of alcohol, should have to fix 'D' plates at both ends of his car. The 'D' would stand for 'Has been drinking' rather than for 'Is drunk'. He would then be restricted to a local journey° and (say) 20 miles an hour. The plates would warn others, and he himself would know that people would be watching him, so he would drive very carefully.

This would be a victory for common sense, freedom *and* safety. Could it not be tried for three years? It would cost the tax-payer nothing.

(Letter from R. Marshall to *The Observer*)

it is all very well: (idiomatic) it is good, but not good enough
urge: encourage
restrict: reduce, cut down
local journey: short trip in the area where you live

from **Application for a driving licence**

Notes to help you	Please complete in INK and BLOCK LETTERS
A business, club or hotel address cannot be accepted unless you live there permanently.	**1. Applicant** (*a*) Surname Christian or forenames (*b*) Mr ☐ Mrs ☐ Miss ☐ Other title, e.g. Dr, Rev. (*c*) Your full permanent address in Great Britain (see note on left).
A provisional driving licence, valid one year. Issued to enable you to drive a motor vehicle, with a view to passing a driving test.	**2. Licence required** (*a*) Please tick box if you have *never* held a British licence (full or provisional°). (*b*) Please tick the type of licence you require Full ☐ Provisional ☐ Duplicate° ☐ Exchange ☐ (*c*) When do you want your new licence to begin? Day...... Month...... Year......
List for question 4(*b*) Driving or attempting to drive while under the influence of drink or drugs. Driving or attempting to drive with an undue° proportion of alcohol in the blood. Failure to provide a specimen of blood for a laboratory test	**4. Disqualifications° and endorsements°** (*a*) Are you disqualified by a court from holding or obtaining a driving licence? Answer YES or NO.........Date and period of disqualification ....Court........... (*b*) Have you been convicted for *any* offence in the last four years (or any offence in the list on the left in the last 11 years) for which any court has ordered an ENDORSEMENT? Answer YES or NO.........If YES give details Date.........Court.........

after driving or attempting to drive a motor vehicle	Offence......... If necessary state other disqualifications/endorsements (or details of successful appeals) on a separate sheet; date it, sign it, and enclose it with this application.
	7. Declaration WARNING You are liable to prosecution° if you knowingly make a false statement to obtain a driving licence. So is anyone else who knowingly makes a false statement to help you obtain one. I declare that I have checked the answers given in this application, that to the best of my knowledge and belief they are correct, and that I am not disqualified by reason of age or otherwise from holding or obtaining the licence for which I am applying. Signature of applicant............... Date.........

(Department of the Environment)

provisional: (see 'Notes to help you') temporary
duplicate: double, i.e. copy
disqualifications: court orders, stopping you from driving
endorsements: court orders, taking away your licence for a certain time
undue: too great
prosecution: facing charges in court

Could you move your elephants?

Barry Norman was a bit thirsty, so he popped in for a quick one° . . . leaving his four elephants tied to parking meters° outside the pub.

Drivers in Tamworth's main street braked and shook their heads with disbelief.

Barry was on his fourth pint when the police came along and arrested him – for being under the influence of liquor° while in charge of an animal. They also ran him in for foul° language.

Norman, a 42-year-old elephant trainer with Sole Bros Circus was fined £20 on both charges.

(*Australian Express*, London)

popped in for a quick one: (colloquial) went for a short drink
parking meter: short steel pole with a clock for measuring parking time
under the influence of liquor: (legal term) drunk
foul: rude

THE MANAGEMENT REGRET
IT HAS BECOME NECESSARY TO
CALL LAST ORDERS AT 10.45
AND CLOSE THE BAR AT 10.50.
PLEASE LEAVE PROMPTLY AT
11.00 p.m. — * — Thank you

(Sign in pub)

NOTICE OF INTENTION TO ENGAGE IN THE SALE OF ALCOHOLIC BEVERAGES

7-22-74
[Insert date posted]

To Whom It May Concern:

Subject to issuance of the license applied for, and commencing not less than 30 days after the date posted, notice is hereby given that the undersigned proposes to sell alcoholic beverages at these premises, described as follows:

☞ *Insert address of premises*

E/S Main St., Jamestown

WARNING

Every person who intentionally defaces, obliterates, tears down or destroys this notice prior to 30 days from the date it was posted is subject to fine or imprisonment in the County Jail (Section 616, Penal Code).

Pursuant to such intention, the undersigned is applying to the Department of Alcoholic Beverage Control for issuance by transfer ~~an original application~~ of an alcoholic beverage license ~~(or licenses)~~ for these premises as follows:

☞ *Specify all licenses applied for as names of licenses appear on application*

Off Sale General
On Sale General Eating Place

Anyone desiring to protest the issuance of such license(s) may file a verified protest with any office of the Department of Alcoholic Beverage Control or Departmental Headquarters, 1215 O Street, Sacramento, California 95814, within 30 days from the date this notice was posted, stating grounds for denial as provided by law. The premises are ~~not~~ now licensed for the sale of alcoholic beverages.

[Name of Applicant] D. R. Hazlewood, M. F. Willey & S. A. Willey

The Consul dropped his eyes at last. How many bottles since then? In how many glasses, how many bottles had he hidden himself, since then alone? Suddenly he saw them, the bottles of aguardiente°, of anís, of jerez, of Highland Queen, the glasses, a babel° of glasses built to the sky, then falling, the glasses toppling and crashing, falling downhill from the Generalife Gardens, the bottles breaking, bottles of Oporto, tinto, blanco, bottles of Pernod, Oxygénée, absinthe, bottles smashing, bottles cast° aside, falling with a thud on the ground in parks, under benches, beds, cinema seats, hidden in drawers at Consulates, bottles of Calvados dropped and broken, or bursting into smithereens°, tossed into garbage° heaps, flung into the sea, the Mediterranean, the Caspian, the Caribbean, bottles floating in the ocean, dead Scotchmen° on the Atlantic highlands – and now he saw them, smelt them, all, from the very beginning – bottles, bottles, bottles, and glasses, glasses, glasses, of bitter, of Dubonnet, of Falstaff, Rye, Johnny Walker, Vieux Whisky, *blanc* Canadien, the apéritifs, the digestifs, the demis, the dobles, the *noch ein* Herr Obers, the bottles, the bottles, the beautiful bottles of tequila, and the gourds°, gourds, gourds, the millions of gourds of beautiful mescal . . . The Consul sat very still. How indeed could he hope to find himself to begin again when, somewhere, perhaps, in one of those lost or broken bottles, in one of those glasses, lay, for ever, the solitary clue° to his identity°? How could he go back and look now, scrabble° among the broken glass, under the eternal bars, under the oceans?

(Malcolm Lowry, *Under the volcano*)

aguardiente, etc . . .: most of the foreign words in this passage are the names of drinks
babel: tower (from the Tower of Babel in the Bible)
cast: thrown
smithereens: tiny pieces
garbage: rubbish
dead Scotchmen: a play on words: (1) Scotch = whisky; (2) dead men = empty bottles
gourds: 'bottles' made of the skin of a large fruit
clue: sign, suggestion
identity: person, i.e. who he is
scrabble: search

Malcolm Lowry – A first impression

I had thrown a blanket over the recumbent° figure, taken off my clothes, and was about to fall into bed when I caught sight of a sheet of paper on which I read, scrawled in my own hand: *Rose in Paris, breakfast here Tuesday.*

My eyes fled to the clock, to the calendar on the wall – and, clutching my aching head, I stifled° a scream.

Rose was my 'little sister', most innocent° and tender-hearted of girls, hardly out of her teens. Rose was a girl who until now had never ventured 'abroad'. Rose was a girl on a visit to an aunt in Paris. Rose was a girl whose Big Brother also lived 'out there'. Rose was a girl who had never had a drink. Rose was a girl who was coming to breakfast ... *any minute.* My head began to reel°. Oh Rose was a girl was a girl was a girl . . .

At last I grew calm. I marched towards my snoring friend. I bent down, put my arms round his waist. Between him and the bathroom lay eight feet of floor: those feet might as well have been miles. I marched into the bathroom, put my head under the cold tap. Without looking in the mirror I began to shave . . .

Oh him? He's a friend ... He isn't feeling very well ... I should leave him ... No, he doesn't like to be touched ... Oh, he's really very nice but – to tell you the truth – he *bites*!

No, that wouldn't do, muttered the shaven face with the aching eyes, when – the doorbell rang, the heart gave a bound, and trembling hands grabbed a pair of trousers and a coat.

'Ah, there you are!'

'I say, you *do* live high up! Mummy sends her love – Oh! – Oh, *look*! What's happened? The poor man! Is he hurt?'

'Not a bit of it, Rose. Come on in – or rather, if you wait one second I'll come out with you. Malcolm won't want to be disturbed – '

'Oh, but the poor man! Why is he on the floor? I'm sure he ought to be in bed?'

'Not a bit of it, he *loves* floors – '

'But he can't be *all right* . . .'

'Perfectly all right. Now I'm ready –'

'But couldn't we lift him? Together? Why does he snore so loud? I'm sure he's *ill* –'

'Not a bit of it, Rose.'

I was dressed, ready, my hand was on the door-knob. 'Look

here, I'll tell you,' I said in exasperation°. 'He has been out celebrating. Yesterday was his – his birthday – and he's just sleeping it off. He'll be –'

'You mean,' asked my little sister, 'you mean he's *drunk*?'

'That's it,' I gasped. 'Drunk. But not disorderly°.'

'Oh dear, how awful!' she groaned, following me down the stairs.

(James Stern, *Encounter*)

recumbent: lying (Malcolm Lowry has spent a long night drinking with the author)
stifled: held back
innocent: not knowing the ways of the world
reel: spin
exasperation: impatience, anger and tiredness
disorderly: badly behaved (being *drunk and disorderly* is a crime for which you can be arrested in Britain)

The Dictator

Although he lived in considerable luxury°, Hitler had few needs. He was indifferent° to the clothes he wore, ate very little, never touched meat, and neither smoked nor drank. He not only kept a special vegetarian° cook to prepare his meals for him, but held strongly that eating meat or any cooked food was a pernicious° habit which had led to the decay of past civilizations. 'There's one thing I can predict to eaters of meat, that the world of the future will be vegetarian.'

The chief reason for Hitler's abstinence seems to have been anxiety about his health. He lived an unhealthy life, with little exercise or fresh air; he took part in no sport, never rode or swam, and he suffered a good deal from stomach disorders. With this went a horror of catching a cold or any form of infection. He was depressed at the thought of dying early, before he had had time to complete his schemes, and he hoped to add years to his life by careful dieting and avoiding alcohol, coffee, tea, and tobacco. In the late-night sessions round the fireplace Hitler never touched stimulants°, not even real tea. He became a crank° as well as a hypochondriac°, and preached° the virtues of vegetarianism to his guests at table with the same insistence as he showed in talking politics.

(Alan Bullock, *Hitler*)

luxury: rich, comfortable surroundings
indifferent (to): uninterested in
vegetarian: person who eats no meat
pernicious: evil and dangerous
stimulant: drug that increases physical or mental activity
crank: person with strange, fixed ideas
hypochondriac: person who is always worried about his health
preached: recommended

Life is a boring business and made more so by those people who preach° moderation in all things. They are a mournful° lot and more of them live on this island than anywhere else. The British are experts at doing everything in moderation, which accounts for our licensing laws°, our hotels which serve dinner between 7.00 p.m. and 8.15 p.m., and the fact that Britons are lousy° lovers. What is more, we go on repeating the old lie that self-denial° is a virtue.

Our attitude to food and drink is that a little of both at the right time of day is all right, but too much of either is disgusting. We are one of the few tribes on this planet that does not regard eating as an occasion to be savoured° with the eyes, the nose and the palate° as well as the belly. We eat and drink without joy because if we didn't we would die.

(Michael Parkinson, from *The Punch guide to good living*)

preach: recommend
mournful: miserable
licensing (laws): times when drinks may be sold
lousy: (colloquial) useless
self-denial: doing without things
savoured: 'tasted', i.e. enjoyed
palate: roof of the mouth, with which one tastes

The Romans thrived on it. The Magyars found great strength in it. But it didn't go down too well with the Turks.

Records have never shown bulls of any sort being used in the making of Bull's Blood wine.

The Hungarian for Bull's Blood, *Egri Bikavér* (Bull's Blood of Eger) refers to the Eger district of Hungary, where the elements have combined in nature to produce conditions which are exactly right for the making of a full-bodied red wine of exceptional strength and character. The Romans were quick to realise this when they occupied the district 17 centuries ago.

But it was when the Magyars settled in the country in the ninth century that the history of Bull's Blood really began. What the Magyars enjoyed more than making wine, was drinking it, and after two centuries of giving themselves up to the grape it seemed the time was about right for the introduction of Christianity.

The later invasion by the Turks did nothing to help life for the Magyars, but one particular incident did much to engrave° Bull's Blood permanently upon the tablets° of Hungarian folklore.

The legend of Bull's Blood

The story concerns the mighty Turkish army of Ali Pasha which had surrounded the ancient walled town of Eger in 1552. The Magyars, though vastly outnumbered° by the Turks, resisted them again and again. The Turks had never met such ferocious° resistance before.

The womenfolk of the town not slow to realise that fighting Turks is thirsty work, were supplying their men with non-stop jugfuls° of Bull's Blood. Eventually the rumour° leaked out° to the Turkish soldiers that the Magyars made themselves fighting mad by drinking the blood of bulls. There was nothing Ali Pasha could do to prevent his soldiers from turning tail and running.

(Advertisement for Egri Bikavér, Bull's Blood)

thrived: lived well
engrave: cut (into stone, wood or metal)

tablets: literally, stone slabs; here it means records
outnumbered: had many more soldiers
ferocious: violent
jugfuls: large containers
rumour: news
leaked out: escaped

Symposium, which now means a learned discussion, in Greek times meant a drinking-party. High thinking was, however, far from being° neglected. In fact the purest gems° of philosophy, among them Plato's *Symposium*, originated in these enjoyable gatherings. The Greeks got more inspiration° from their wine cups than we get from our tea cups.

(F. Roberts, *Medical terms, their origin and construction*)

far from being: not at all
gems: (literally = precious stones) fine thoughts
inspiration: good ideas

11 The green years

A child born today in the UK stands a 10 times greater chance of being admitted° to a mental hospital than to a university . . . This can be taken as an indication that we are driving our children mad more effectively than we are genuinely educating them. Perhaps it is our very way of educating them that is driving them mad.

(R. D. Laing, *The politics of experience*)

admitted: sent to

At eight in the morning a child rang the bell. Half an hour later, 'through fog, rain, or the slanting rays of the autumn sun,' the little muzhiks° appeared by twos and threes, swinging their empty arms. As in the previous years, they brought no books or notebooks with them – nothing at all, save° the desire to learn. The classrooms were painted pink and blue. In one, mineral samples, dried plants, and physics apparatus lined the shelves. But no books. Why no books? The pupils came to the classroom as though it were home; they sat where they liked, on the floor, on the window-ledge, on a chair or the corner of a table, they listened or they did not listen to what the teacher was saying, drew near when he said something that interested them, left the room when work or play called them elsewhere – but were silenced by their fellow pupils at the slightest sound. The lessons – if these casual° chats° between an adult and some children could be called that – went on from eight thirty to noon and from three to six in the afternoon. Those who lived too far away to go home at night slept in the school. In the summer they sat around their teacher outdoors in the grass.

As a disciple° of Jean-Jacques Rousseau°, Tolstoy wanted to believe that human nature was basically good, that all evil was a product of civilization and that the teacher must not smother° the child under the weight of learning, but must help him, little by little, to shape his own personality.

(Henry Troyat, *Tolstoy* – a biography)

muzhiks: Russian farm workers' children
save: except for
casual: friendly, informal
chats: talks
disciple: follower
J. J. Rousseau: eighteenth-century French philosopher
smother: kill the child's interest

The green years

[This story is set in South Africa. Lee is a young African who makes his living by doing various small jobs in homes and offices. Here he is talking to a Jewish girl in the office.]

'Lee.'
I stopped and turned to her.
'That is your name, isn't it?'
'Yes, missus.'
'Miss, not missus. You only say missus to a married woman.'
Her smile encouraged° me.
'We say it to all white women.'
'Then you are wrong. Say miss.'
'Yes, miss.'
'That's better . . . Tell me, how old are you?'
'Going on for eleven, miss.'
'Why don't you go to school?'
'I don't know, miss.'
'Don't you want to?'
'I don't know, miss.'
'Can you read or write?'
'No, miss.'
'Stop saying miss now.'
'Yes, miss.'
She laughed.

'So you can't read?'

'No, miss.'

'Wouldn't you like to?'

'I don't know, miss.'

'Want to find out?'

'Yes, miss.'

She turned the pages of the book in front of her. She looked at me, then began to read from *Lamb's Tales from Shakespeare*.

The story of Othello jumped at me and invaded° my heart and mind as the young woman read. I was transported to the land where the brave Moor° lived and loved and destroyed his love.

The young woman finished.

'Like it?'

'Oh yes!'

'Good. This book is full of stories like that. If you go to school you'll be able to read them for yourself.'

'Then I'm going to school!'

'When?'

'Monday.'

'I've started something!' She laughed. 'But why didn't you go before?'

'Nobody told me.'

'You must have seen other children go to school.'

'Nobody told me about the stories.'

'Oh yes, the stories.'

'When I can read and write I'll make stories like that!'

(Peter Abrahams, from *Modern African prose*, ed. Richard Rive)

encouraged: gave him the strength to go on talking
invaded: rushed into
Moor: Othello

'I want to write a letter to Mom,' Chris says.

That sounds good to me. I go to the desk and get some paper. I bring it to Chris and give him my pen. That brisk° morning air has given him some energy too. He puts the paper in front of him, grabs the pen in a heavy grip and then concentrates on the blank paper for a while.

He looks up. 'What day is it?'

I tell him. He nods and writes it down.

Then I see him write, 'Dear Mom:'

Then he stares at the paper for a while.

Then he looks up. 'What should I say?'

We're interrupted by the hot cakes and I tell him to put the letter to one side and I'll help him afterward.

When we are done, Chris brings out the paper again. 'Now help me,' he says.

'Okay,' I say. I tell him getting stuck is the commonest trouble of all. Usually, I say, your mind gets stuck when you're trying to do too many things at once. What you have to do is try not to force words to come. That just gets you more stuck. What you have to do now is separate out the things and do them one at a time. You're trying to think of what to *say* and what to say *first* at the same time, and that's too hard. So separate them out. Just make a list of all the things you want to say in any old order. Then later we'll figure out° the right order.

'Like what things?' he asks.

'Well, what do you want to tell her?'

'About the trip.'

'What things about the trip?'

He thinks for a while. 'About the mountains we climbed.'

'Okay, write that down,' I say.

He does.

Then I see him write down another item, then another, while I finish my cigarette and coffee. He goes through three sheets of paper, listing things he wants to say.

'I'll never get all this into one letter,' he says.

He sees me laugh, and frowns.

I say, 'Just pick out the best things.' Then we head outside and onto the motorcycle again.

(Robert Pirsig, *Zen and the art of motorcycle maintenance*)

brisk: sharp
figure out: decide on

Mary had a little lamb,
Its fleece° was white as snow,
And everywhere that Mary went
Her lamb was sure to go.

(Traditional – nursery rhyme)

fleece: wool

Mary had a little lamb,
Her father shot it dead,
And now it goes to school with her
Between two chunks° of bread.

(Modern version, sung by schoolchildren)

(I. & P. Opie, *The lore and language of School-children*)

chunks: pieces

A friend of mine had seen her 16-year-old son mooning around° the house all holiday and finally decided she'd cheer him up by offering to decorate his bedroom any colour he liked. He smiled a faint smile at this. 'What colour would you like?' she asked him. 'Black,' he said. 'Don't be stupid, you can't have a *black* room.' 'There you go,' he said with a hollow laugh, 'I can't have anything I want, can I? You don't care . . .'

(Judith Cook, *The Guardian*)

mooning around: lying about, not knowing what to do

'A very quick-tempered girl once made a tremendous scene and then slammed the door as she left the room. Her father calmly called her back and asked her to close the door quietly. She walked out and slammed the door again, and the whole scene was repeated once more.

But her father still remained calm, called her back yet again and then gently lifted the door off its hinges° and placed it against the wall. The girl was speechless°, calmed down at once, and the normal good relationship between father and daughter was able to run its course° once more . . .'

The moral for teachers is that they should give pupils an occasional dose° of the unexpected. A normally calm teacher should sometimes fly off the handle° and a bad-tempered one should discipline herself to occasional displays of iron self-control.

(*Observer Review*)

hinges: small pieces of metal on which the door hangs
speechless: silent
run its course: go on
dose: amount (usually of medicine)
fly off the handle: (idiomatic) get angry

School rules anger boys

A headmaster is to look into complaints of sex discrimination° at a mixed comprehensive° school. The boys claim that they are called by their surnames° while the girls are always addressed by their christian° names – and the boys have to stand in assembly° while the girls are given chairs.

Mr Peter Chambers, head of the Rushcliffe Comprehensive School, said he has agreed to hold informal talks with the staff°.

(*The Guardian*)

discrimination: making (unfair) differences (between boys and girls)
mixed comprehensive: large school for both sexes
surnames: family names
christian (names): first names
assembly: meeting in the morning before school begins
staff: teachers

Recollections

Monday evening. Me reading, my brother making an aeroplane. Phone rings and my mother answered it. Cheerful hallo then her face all white and her voice all wobbly°. Put the phone down. Silence then – Ricky (my cousin aged nine) had been run over on this foggy November evening, his skull crushed, died in the ambulance.

We sat all that evening almost in silence. Nobody cried. Everyone was isolated° in shock each sitting alone on his chair. I remember Renee my aunt kept saying – everyone must do as they feel best for them but somehow it was better to all just sit there. There was some comfort in the presence of all sharing this calamity°. My memory of that evening is sharp – those pale faces strained but still. Kind of waiting – perhaps to wake up from a bad dream.

Next morning I decided to go to school because there seemed no point in staying at home. I walked along the familiar back streets as if seeing them for the first time. These houses, shops, traffic lights I knew – never noticed but I saw them differently. How could they remain unmoved when some bit of my life was shattered°. Why were they the same when this had happened – but look so different as I stared out of the bony holes in my head. At school I had to meet my friends. They did not know. I sat behind my desk lid not saying anything at all. After prayers I walked with a friend across the grounds. I told her and for the first time started to cry. She went to her biology lesson. I sat on a seat until I stopped crying and finally went to my lesson. I must have been about half an hour late. The teacher said nothing. I wondered why. Usually one was asked.

I don't remember much about the next few days. We read through all the letters of consolation and awarded each a certain amount of points – points being taken off for clichés° like 'wherever he is, he is happy now'. These made me angry for to me he was nowhere, finished. He had been but had gone out like a candle.

The funeral was awful. The whole family squabbles° about the order in which people should go – does a second cousin go before a something-in-law. It seemed so incredibly mean and stupid. Wreathes and bouquets°. One woman had sent a wreath to Ricky from her dog. This nearly sent me crazy. It seemed like playing with this child's death.

We went to the crematorium° scared as hell. Tense. Didn't know what to expect. A man in black came up to us carrying what looked like a giant salt-pot. Where do you want the ashes shaken? He didn't wait for explanations or questions. Quick as a flash he moved to the nearest bushes. Shake shake with the pot. Good morning, a bow and was gone.

Silence. Stephen laughed once. Stopped. Gloria smiled. Suddenly we three were laughing hysterically – the sort of laughing that hurts your ribs, that dies down for a while then starts again, never to end.

This was death, this ludicrous° shaking a salt-pot. We had expected something tragic. This insulted us totally and yet was a relief. It was a commercial transaction° – no mystery. The man had many shakings to do in the morning – it was his job.

(Judith, aged 20, *Understanding children writing*)

wobbly: shaky
isolated: cut off from the others
calamity: terrible accident
shattered: broken
clichés: words and phrases used so often that they lose their meaning
squabbles: arguments
wreathes and bouquets: flowers
crematorium: where bodies are burnt
ludicrous: absurd, silly
commercial transaction: business deal

On 6 December, Seales was not in his place and I marked him absent°. Just before the end of the lesson he came in and walked briskly° to my table.

'Sorry I can't stay, Sir, but my mother died early this morning and I'm helping my Dad with things.'

As if those words finally broke all his efforts to be strong and grown up, his face crumpled and he wept like the small boy he really felt. I got up quickly and led him unresisting to my chair, where he sat, his head in his hands, sobbing° bitterly.

I gave the news to the class: they received it in shocked silence, in that immediate sympathy and compassion which only the young seem to know and experience, and then many of them were weeping too.

(E. R. Braithwaite, *To sir, with love*)

absent: away
briskly: quickly
sobbing: crying

[From a review of children's books]

The least professionally packaged° volume of the three is *Once upon a time I love you.* It appears to have been put together by a number of somehow related people of varying ages, and has a great deal of material cramped° into its 56 pages. Good intentions and honest effort have clearly gone into this endeavour°. It commendably° tries to tell kids that being who you are is valuable and doing what you do is important, but it never really lets go of an adult approach long enough to find what kids will accept or find exciting. I mean to say, a monster° who gets a kiss from a beautiful little girl and turns into an 'outstanding citizen in his community'?! I'm not quarrelling with the way this transformation° works – I just don't think it's as neat as turning into a handsome prince°, and neither, I suspect, will kids.

The poetry in the book shows a little more imagination than the good-citizen stories, and even has some fun with words and line structure. Some of it is the kind of stuff that adults will smile at and think is adorable° long after their kids have decided it's silly.

(Books in Canada)

packaged: prepared, presented
cramped: crushed
endeavour: effort
commendably: for reasons worth admiring
monster: frightening creature, often half-beast, half-man
transformation: great change
. . . prince: in most fairy stories the monster turns into a good-looking prince
adorable: (ironic) delightful, lovely

Child's guide to male chauvinism°

'Aunty sits on the sands with Jane and the dog, and Peter is in the water with Uncle. "Are you too hot, dear?" Aunty asks Jane . . . Peter calls to Jane and Aunty, "Come into the water with us."

Poor Jane, what a weed° she is. She wears a white dress and never gets dirty. You can see her at the back of the picture, sitting quietly with her hands folded in her lap. 'Peter is in the water with his new boat in his hand . . . "It was good of Uncle to buy you a new boat," says Jane . . . "Yes," says Peter, "and it was nice of Aunty to let you have her old doll. I hope you like it."'

Of course she does. She's everything a female child is supposed to be. She is also one of the main characters in a Reading Scheme used in 68 % of British primary schools. Successive° generations of children grow up with Peter and Jane as their most familiar fictional characters, their models of boyhood and girlhood. They're not just learning to read, they're learning how to behave.

The series is, however, gradually being updated°. In the first book of the modernised series Peter and Jane go into a toy shop. Peter buys a mechanical toy like he did in the earlier edition; Jane buys a doll, but this time (ah, progress!) it is a black one. The text continues: 'Peter has a ball, Peter likes the ball.' The picture shows Peter kicking the ball and Jane standing by, watching. The ball gets caught in a tree. In the earlier edition, Peter climbed the tree alone. Now Jane climbs with him. But who is higher up the tree fetching the ball? No prizes for guessing.

The new books have busier settings than the old. Even so, they bear little relation to the lives of most schoolchildren. On the whole, male and female characters are still cast° in traditional roles and behave in predictably° 'masculine' and 'feminine' ways. From classics to comics, it's the same story. Males pursue complex adventures full of action and excitement, alone or in all-male groups, or leading their female companions. Females have quieter, cosier° lives. Things happen to them. Males *make* things happen. There are exceptions, of course, but most of these books are imported from Scandinavia and the United States.

The only scheme which, in later volumes, appears to have made a conscious effort to avoid sex stereotyping° is *Breakthrough to Literacy*, in which, for instance, we find Dad collecting his son from school and making the tea while Mum is at work.

Should publishers change their ways? Should they encourage writers to produce less biased° material? It is often argued in defence of the present situation that current publications mirror reality; they show life as it is, with Mum in the kitchen and Dad reading the newspaper. But so many of the books I've seen *exaggerate*°: they ignore the variety and complexity of real life.

(Anna Coote, *The Sunday Times Magazine*)

chauvinism: belief that oneself (or one's group) is superior or special
weed: child with no spirit
successive: one after the other
updated: changed to suit present taste
cast: placed
predictably: as might be expected
cosier: softer, more comfortable
stereotyping: fitting into a fixed pattern or type
biased: prejudiced
exaggerate: go too far, i.e. make life seem too simple

Pooh builds a house

'I've been thinking,' said Pooh, 'and what I've been thinking is this. I've been thinking about Eeyore.'

'What about Eeyore?'

'Well, poor Eeyore has nowhere to live.'

'Nor he has°,' said Piglet.

'*You* have a house, Piglet, and I have a house, and they are very good houses. And Christopher Robin has a house, and Owl and Kanga and Rabbit have houses, and even Rabbit's friends and relations have houses or somethings, but poor Eeyore has nothing. So what I've been thinking is: Let's build him a house.'

'That,' said Piglet, 'is a Grand Idea. Where shall we build it?'

'We will build it here,' said Pooh, 'just by this wood, out of the wind, because this is where I thought of it. And we will call this Pooh Corner. And we will build an Eeyore House with sticks at Pooh Corner for Eeyore.'

(A. A. Milne, *The house at Pooh Corner*)

nor he has: you're right, he hasn't

[Winnie the Pooh is a toy bear, Eeyore is a donkey.]

'And this snow,' Robert Jordan said, 'You think there will be much?'

'Much,' said Pablo contentedly. Then called to Pilar. 'You don't like it woman, either. Now that you command you do not like this snow?'

'*A mi que*?' Pilar said over her shoulder. 'If it snows it snows.'

'Drink some wine, *Inglés*,' Pablo said. 'I have been drinking all day waiting for the snow.'

'Give me a cup,' Robert Jordan said.

'To the snow,' Pablo said and touched cups with him. Robert Jordan looked him in the eyes and clinked his cup. You bleary°-eyed murderous sod°, he thought. I'd like to clink this cup against your teeth. *Take it easy*, he told himself, *take it easy*.

'It is very beautiful the snow,' Pablo said. 'You won't want to sleep outside with the snow falling.'

(E. Hemingway, *For whom the bell tolls*)

bleary: red, tired
sod: brute

According to a new publishing company, Enfance Publishing, 'every leading author has at least one children's book in him.' *Every* leading author?

From **THE POOH ALSO RISES**
by Ernest Hemingway

It snowed hard that winter. It was the winter they all went up to the Front. You could get up early in the morning, if you were not wounded and forced to lie on your bed and look at the ceiling and wonder about the thing with the women, and you could see them going up to the Front in the snow. When they walked in the snow, they left tracks, and after they had gone the snow would come down again and pretty soon the tracks would not be there any more. That is the way it is with snow.

Pooh did not go up to the Front that winter. Nor did he lie in bed and look at the ceiling, although last winter he had lain in bed and looked up at the ceiling, because that was the winter he had gone up to the Front and got his wound. It had snowed that winter, too.

This winter he could walk around. It was one of those wounds that left you able to walk around. It was one of those wounds that did not leave you much more.

Pooh got up and he went out into the snow and he went to see Piglet. Piglet was sitting at his usual table, looking at an empty glass of *enjarda*°.

'I thought you were out,' said Pooh.

'No,' said Piglet. 'I was not out.'

'You were thinking about the wound?' said Pooh.

'No,' said Piglet. 'I was not thinking about the wound. I do not think about the wound very much any more.'

'We could go and see Eeyore,' said Pooh.

'Yes,' said Piglet, 'We could go and see Eeyore.'

When they got to Eeyore's house, he was looking at an empty glass of *ortega*°. They used to make *ortega* by taking the new *orreros*° out of the ground very early in the morning, and crushing them between the *mantemagni*°, but they did not make it that way any more. Not since the fighting up at the Front.

'Do you hear the guns?' said Eeyore.

'Yes,' said Pooh. 'I hear the guns.'

'It is still snowing,' said Piglet.

'Yes,' said Eeyore. 'That is the way it is.'

'That is the way it is,' said Pooh.

(Alan Coren, *The sanity inspector*)

enjarda, ortega, etc.: words invented by the author to sound like Spanish words

Employment of children and young people

The employment of a child is prohibited° until he has attained the age of 13 (unless authority° is given in local by-laws for him to be employed by his parent or guardian in light agricultural work). From the age of 13, while still at school, he may not be employed before the close of school hours on any day on which he is required to attend school; before seven o'clock in the morning or after seven o'clock in the evening of any day; for more than two hours on any day on which he is required to attend school or on any Sunday; nor may he be required to lift, carry or move anything so heavy as might injure him.

(COI pamphlet, *Children in Britain*)

prohibited: not allowed
authority: permission

'Just think, you'll be leaving school in a few weeks, starting your first job, meeting fresh people. That's something to look forward to, isn't it?'

Bill looked past him without replying.

'Have you got a job yet?'

'No, sir. I've to see t'youth employment bloke° this afternoon.'

'What kind of job are you after?'

'I'm not bothered°. Owt'll do° me.'

'You'll try to get something that interests you, though?'

'I shan't have much choice, shall I? I shall have to take what they've got.'

'I thought you'd have been looking forward to leaving.'

'I'm not bothered.'

'I thought you didn't like school.'

'I don't, but that don't mean that I'll like work, does it? Still, I'll get paid for not liking it, that's one thing.'

'Yes. Yes, I suppose it is.'

Mr Farthing shook his head slightly and looked at his watch.

(Barry Hines, *Kes*)

t(he) youth employment bloke: the man who helps young people find jobs
I'm not bothered: I don't care
Owt'll do: (dialect) anything will do

What's it like to be 16?

Teenagers were interviewed from two comprehensive schools, one near Oxford, the other in Sheffield. Some are unemployed, others are working or about to start their studies. Here are their views on work.

Barry: 'I'm an apprentice° in a fairly big company. £17 a week. Not bad really. I enjoy it. I'll stay there and become a skilled plumber°. The first year's going to be the worst. They give me all the nasty things to do. I have to clean up all the drains and the tools. All they do is tell you what to do and sit around watching you – but they're quite nice people. I even have to shut my boss's car door for him . . .'

Tina: 'When I left school I wanted to get a full-time job. I wanted some money to save up and to bring into the house. I've written off to at least 21 places. Some of them didn't bother to reply. They promised to tell me or ring me up, but just didn't bother. It gets me° when they do that. You go for an interview and they say "I'll ring you before half past twelve." You sit there and the phone never rings. I'd love to get a job. I'm fed up really. I go down to the careers office° once a week. They've given me papers to look at but they've been no good to me. I've got a typewriter at home and I'm teaching myself to type.'

Richard: 'I want a job out of doors, not down the pit° or on a factory floor. I'd really like to be a vet°. I know it's difficult training and you would need qualifications. I might feel different when I'm older, but I'm sick of exams at the moment. As long as I don't sit around the house all day and I'm going to interviews, my parents wouldn't put the pressure on°. They know I'm trying.'

Michael: 'My mother found me my job. It's at the garage where my Dad gets the car serviced°. I earn about £13 a week, and half of that goes to my mother for my keep°. One day I hope to own my own garage.'

Susan: 'I tried for about 10 or 11 jobs and I went to this jeweller's shop°, but I bite my nails so they said no.'

Shaun: 'I would like to go to an agricultural college. My parents want me to get a decent job – not one where I wish I hadn't taken the job and have to come back to them. Something with security.'

Stephen: 'My Dad's a plumber and I'd like to take after him because he's got a car and everything. When my Dad was a kid he could go out of one job and into the next. He told me you can't do it any more because there's so many out of work.'

Gary: 'I had one job helping a plasterer°, but it was too hard. You had to run up six flights of stairs with two buckets of cement, run down and start again. I was going to join the Army, because I couldn't get a job, but Ulster° put me off. My Mum wouldn't have let me go anyway.'

(*The Sunday Times Magazine*)

apprentice: person learning a trade
plumber: man who works with water pipes
(it) gets (me): (colloquial) annoys
careers office: place where young people get advice about jobs
pit: mine
vet: veterinary surgeon, i.e. animal doctor
put the pressure on: (colloquial) try to force him (to get a job)
serviced: checked
keep: living expenses
jeweller's shop: place where rings, watches, etc. are sold
plasterer: man who covers walls so that they can be painted
Ulster: Northern Ireland

12 Short tales and tall stories

The pig that did fly

Aeroplanes heading for London yesterday were warned to look out for . . . a flying pig.

The pilot of a light aircraft first spotted it over the city at 2,000 metres and radioed Heathrow°: 'You're not going to believe this, but . . .'

Then West Drayton air traffic control centre picked it up° on radar°. A police helicopter was called in and followed the pig over London Bridge. And the London Electricity Board was warned in case the pig came down on one of its pylons°.

It reached 6,000 metres over Chatham and eventually landed on a farm at Chilham, Kent – where it burst.

It turned out to be a 13 metre pink balloon, which was made to advertise a concert by the pop group Pink Floyd, but broke free while being tied between the chimneys of Battersea Power Station.

Pity, really . . .

(*Daily Mail*)

Heathrow: London's largest airport
picked it up: saw it
radar: a machine that shows the position of, e.g. ships, aeroplanes, rockets, etc.
pylons: large steel structures that carry electricity wires

SUNDAY EXTRA
AIR BI
martin
" Incidentally, did you try that local brandy on the Bangkok stopover ? "

As I sat under the apple tree,
A birdie sent his love to me,
And as I wiped it from my eye,
I said, Thank goodness, cows can't fly.

(I. & P. Opie, *The lore and language of school-children*)

*

I never saw a purple cow
I hope I'll never see one,
But I can tell you anyhow
I'd rather see than be one.

Bitten by 'shark-toothed' frog

Mrs Nella van Niewenhuisen, a 69-year-old housewife, had two stitches in her hand after a frog 'with teeth like a shark's°' attacked her.

The bite tore out a piece of skin and left a wound a little smaller than a matchbox in size. The frog had jaws lined with sharp spikes, sloping backwards, like a shark's teeth.

Mrs van Niewenhuisen was working in her garden when she suddenly heard a snap and felt a burning pain in her right hand. She jerked it back and the frog, still hanging on, went flying through the air. But the moment it hit the ground it charged back at her. She shrieked°, rolled over and jumped to her feet.

Her son came to investigate and the frog went for him° as well. It was then caught and killed, and given to the local pharmacist° for preservation.

(Newspaper report)

shark: large fish with big jaws and sharp teeth
shrieked: screamed
went for him: attacked him
pharmacist: person who sells medicine and toilet articles

'Human fly' built house in steelwork under bridge

HOUSTON. BRITISH COLUMBIA. Police are looking for a 'human fly' who apparently built and occupied a house in the steelwork under a highway overpass°. The overpass carries Highway 16 over the Bulkley River and the Canadian National Railways Line.

The house, built between two 2-metre girders° more than 15 metres above the river, is 'really well constructed', said Mr Jack Turford of the BC Highways Department. The occupant – possibly a woman – would have to be a human fly to reach it, he added.

Bridge workers tried to reach the house by swinging over the side of the bridge and were 'absolutely petrified'°. There is apparently no way of reaching the house either from the end of the bridge or by swinging over the side. The bridge workers finally used the Houston Fire Department's ladder to reach it.

The worker who entered the house found a 2-metre by 3-metre home, insulated° with 3-centimetre thick foam plastic and fitted with a battery operated lighting system. He also found a stove but no sign of food. Wooden planks placed across another girder were used as a toilet. A roll of toilet paper was also found.

Mr Turford said the builder could be a woman because a worker recently saw a woman climbing over the bridge railing.

The house will be pulled down because it is a safety hazard° to anyone trying to reach it.

(*Toronto Globe & Mail*)

overpass: bridge
girders: steel supports
petrified: terrified
insulated: protected from the cold
hazard: danger

When Cathy was lying dead in her big bed with her family all around her, and a lot of great performers they were too – Flora Robson, Geraldine Fitzgerald, Hugh Williams – all weeping° silently, I glanced nervously at the instructions in my script°.

(Edgar breaks down at foot of bed and sobs°.)

'Willie,' I whispered, 'I can't do that.'

'Do what?'

'Sob. I don't know how to.'

'Speak up.'

'I don't know how to sob, Willie.'

'Speak up, louder.'

'I DON'T KNOW HOW TO SOB,' I yelled.

Wyler addressed the whole set°. 'Well, you've all heard it – here's an actor who says he doesn't know how to act . . . now . . . SOB.'

I tried and it was pretty grisly°. I tried again.

'Jesus,' said Wyler, 'can you make a crying face?'

I made some sort of squashed-up grimace.°

'Oh, God,' he groaned. '*Irving*!' Irving Sindler was instantly at his side. 'Give him the blower, Irving,' said Wyler.

Through a handkerchief, Sindler puffed menthol° into my open eyes.

'Bend over the corpse°,' said Wyler. 'Now make your crying face . . . Blink your eyes . . . Squeeze a little . . . Bend over the corpse.'

A terrible thing happened. Instead of tears coming out of my eyes, green slime° came out of my nose.

'Ooh! How *horrid*!' shrieked the corpse, shot out of bed and disappeared at high speed into her dressing-room.

(David Niven, *The moon's a balloon*)

weeping: crying
script: actor's words
sobs: cries (softly)
set: actors, technicians, etc.
grisly: bad
grimace: an ugly expression on the face
menthol: gas (to make him cry)
corpse: dead body
slime: a nasty substance

Handicap

BUSINESSMAN Isao Takahashi was killed when lightening struck the metal zip on his trousers while he was playing golf in Kyoto, Japan, yesterday.

(*The Guardian*)

Hands off!

A Moroccan handball team has been banned° for life because they beat up the referee every time he awarded points to their opponents.

(*Sunday Mirror*)

banned: forbidden to play

Did the ref.° hiccup°

COLOMBO: The Football Federation here has decided to breathalyse° soccer referees before kick-off time. This follows some recent allegations° that some referees have been 'deeply under the influence of liquor' while on the field of play.

(*Sunday Express*)

ref.: referee
hiccup: a noise often made by drunk men
breathalyse: test the breath to find out if a person has been drinking
allegations: claims

Soccer° attack

BRAZZAVILLE. Cameroun soldiers rushed onto the field and attacked the Congolese National Soccer team a few minutes before the end of Sunday's match against the Cameroun in Yaoundé, Brazzaville Radio said yesterday.

The radio said the team had been rushed back to Brazzaville in President Marien Ngouabi's personal plane and taken to hospital. Two players, the trainer and the team doctor, were seriously injured.

(*Sydney Morning Herald*)

soccer: football

(*The Sunday Times*, Johannesburg)

Inside the Cage!

This is the Cage – one football club's short, sharp answer to soccer hooliganism°.

It is about as comfortable as Colditz° and just as hard to get out of. And, say officials of Orient who built it this season, it works.

Fans° who have caused trouble are taken away by the police and put into the Cage until after the game is over. In the old days, a fan who was thrown out of the stadium often paid his money again, came back in and started more trouble. Orient secretary, Peter Barnes, said: 'One supporter holds the record for being kicked out of the ground three times during the same match. But since we built the Cage, no one has been in it more than once. If they land up° there, they miss the game of course – and have to stand in the cold and rain instead.'

Fans are kept in the Cage for anything from using abusive° language to picking fights with rival fans. Orient have little trouble with their own supporters, said Mr Barnes. Most of the Cage's guests are visiting fans. 'We put up barbed wire° and built a special hut for the policemen who guard them, so that the officers can keep warm while the troublemakers stay cold. It makes them think twice,' he said.

The barbed-wire cage has already become part of football folklore in London's East End. It even has its own chant°: 'If you don't behave, we'll put you in the Cage – you naughty boy!'

(*The Sun*)

hooliganism: bad behaviour: fighting, throwing bottles, etc.
Colditz: prisoner of war camp which was extremely difficult to escape from
fans: supporters (of the football teams)
land up: are put inside
abusive: rude
barbed wire: fence with small sharp bits of wire sticking out
chant: song

English country gents° often hunt birds, and no one objected when Sheikh Zaid Ben Sultan, ruler of Abu Dhabi, decided to try his hand° at the sport at his luxurious° English country home. What distressed° neighbours was that he used a machine gun.

(Newsweek, quoted in 'Sayings of the Year,' *The Guardian*)

gents: gentlemen
try his hand: see how well he could shoot
luxurious: expensive
distressed: disturbed

What is black and shiny and lives in trees and is dangerous?
A crow with a submachine gun

HUNTED!

A breathless man staggers towards the end of a four-mile manhunt. On his heels come a pack of bloodhounds°. But the man hunted by the dogs is no common criminal running for his life.

He is one of 'the professionals' from Britain's modern army.

The manhunt was used as a training exercise for Guards at Pirbright, Surrey.

Labour MP° Mr Frank Allaun is furious about the incident. 'It seems to me distasteful and disgraceful,' he said.

Young Guards in training were paid £1 to run about four miles with a pack of bloodhounds in hot pursuit°.

An Army spokesman said that 100 to 150 recruits° took part in the manhunt. Three were used as human quarries°; the rest did their best to keep up with the hounds and huntsmen.

Master of the Hunt, Major Bill Stringer, said that all the men were volunteers°. 'You'd be surprised how many people like being hunted,' he said. 'I normally ask the quarry not to bathe the day before. That makes the scent nice and rich.'

A legal officer for the National Council for Civil Liberties said: 'I wouldn't have thought there's very much benefit to be had from training a man like this.'

But an Army spokesman said: 'The recruits would have done a run normally, but this was something that seemed rather more interesting for them.'

The last word on the manhunt came from a 19-year-old Irish Guardsman, one of the human quarries: 'They always say that in the Army you don't volunteer for anything,' he said. 'It's a bloody hard way of getting some extra beer money.'

(*Sunday Mirror*)

bloodhounds: hunting dogs
MP: Member of Parliament
pursuit: chase
recruits: men who have just entered the Army
quarry: the 'animals' being chased
volunteers: men who chose freely (to be hunted)

The way in which the army recruitment campaign° has been developed over the last years is most impressive. Against a diminishing° likelihood° of world war; against diminishing patriotism°; against diminishing acceptance of authority, the army has done a remarkable job. I do not believe that there is anyone who would not be proud to have been associated with a campaign as effective and creative as that of 'The Professionals'. You may like to know that 'The Professionals' campaign in 1975–76 brought in 31,437 enquiries at a cost per reply of £26.5. Over 15,000 enlistments° were secured at a cost per enlistment of £53.5. In other words, there was a 50% conversion°, which is excellent by anyone's standards.

(From speech given by Graeme Roe, vice-president of Roe Downton Advertising Agency, London)

campaign: publicity drive
diminishing: getting smaller
likelihood: possibility
patriotism: love of the motherland
enlistments: persons joining the army
conversion: acceptance

A Fresno Fable

A short story by William Saroyan

Kerope Antoyan, the grocer, ran into Aram Bashmanian, the lawyer, in the street one day and said: 'Aram, you are the very man I have been looking for. It is a miracle° that I find you this way at this time, because there is only one man in this world I want to talk to, and you are that man, Aram.'

'Very well, Kerope,' the lawyer said. 'Here I am.'

'This morning,' the grocer said, 'when I got up I said to myself, "if there is anybody in this whole world I can trust, it is Aram", and here you are before my eyes – my salvation°, the restorer of peace to my soul. If I had hoped to see an angel° in the street, I would not have been half so pleased as I am to see you, Aram.'

'Well, of course, I can always be found in my office,' Aram

said, 'but I'm glad we have met in the street. What is it, Kerope?'

'Aram, we are from Bitlis°. We understand all too well that before one speaks one thinks. Before the cat tastes the fish, his whiskers° must feel the head. A prudent° man does not open an umbrella for one drop of rain. Caution with strangers, care with friends, trust in one's very own – as *you* are my very own, Aram. I thank God for bringing you to me at this moment of crisis.'

'What is it, Kerope?'

'Aram, every eye has a brow, every lip a moustache, the foot wants its shoe, the hand its glove, what is a tailor without his needle, even a lost dog remembers having had a bone, until a candle is lighted a prayer for a friend cannot be said, one man's ruin is another man's reward.'

'Yes, of course, but what is the crisis, Kerope?'

'A good song in the mouth of a bad singer is more painful to the ear than a small man's sneeze°,' the grocer said.

'Kerope,' the lawyer said, 'How can I help you?'

'You are like a brother to me, Aram – a younger brother whose wisdom is far greater than my own, far greater than any man's.'

'Well, thank you, Kerope,' Aram said, 'but *please* tell me what's the matter, so I can try to help you.'

In the end, though, Kerope refused to tell Aram his problem.

Moral°: If you're really smart°, you won't trust even an angel.

(From *The Sunday Telegraph Magazine*)

miracle: wonderful, unexpected chance
salvation: rescue
angel: good spirit, said to live with God
Bitlis: town in Turkey (Armenia). Both men are living far away from their native land
whiskers: strong hairs on the side of the face
prudent: careful, wise
sneeze: sudden noise made through the nose (as when you have a cold)
moral: lesson, teaching. This story is an imitation of traditional folk tales, which usually end with a simple observation
smart: clever